The Appointed Times

A Paper by
Randy Bullock
Illinois, U.S.A.

"For the vision is yet for the appointed time;
It hastens toward the goal, and it will not fail.
Though it tarries, wait for it;
For it will certainly come, it will not delay."

Habakkuk 2:3

Copyright © 1996

The Appointed Times

Randy Bullock, Illinois, U.S.A.

**Published in 1996 from the original manuscript
which was completed and first made available
in June 1995**

Quotations are from
The Holy Bible, New American Standard
Copyright © The Lockman Foundation, 1960, 1962, 1963, 1971, 1973, 1975, 1977

ISBN: 0 9526793 1 0

Printed in Great Britain by the Commerical Centre, Oldham, Lancs.

Published in Great Britain by Tony MacCormack
P.O. Box 29 , Wilmslow, Cheshire. SK9 1FD

FOREWORD

Second to the Bible, this is the most fascinating and intriguing book I have ever read. It may be the most timely and profound commentary now available on God's revelation concerning the end of the age.

I have had the unusual privilege of getting to know the author and his lovely family. Randy Bullock is a balanced, very hard-working business and family man who has a great love for God and a deep respect for God's holy Word, the Bible. With a quick, analytical mind, Randy is a relentless seeker of truth and a tireless researcher. He may labour many days over one linguistic or historical point, seemingly minor to many of us, but nothing, not one jot or tittle, in God's revealed truth is minor to Randy. I cannot guarantee that every single detail of Randy's work is perfectly correct, but I will guarantee that each came from much prayerful and diligent study.

It is noteworthy that Randy approaches his study without the usual traditional theological or denominational presuppositions that might distort or bias his conclusions. Yet he has considered and reviewed the opinions of many scholars of various persuasions. The guiding principle of his quest has been: *"What did God say, and what does God mean?"*

Randy Bullock is also a man of humble and contrite heart, not seeking his own glory or gain, but always only God's glory. I am reminded of God's words to Isaiah: *"This is the one I esteem: He who is humble and contrite in spirit, and trembles at my word".* (66:2).

The many biblical signs and prophecies being fulfilled overwhelmingly point to the end of the age and the very, very soon return of the Lord Jesus Christ. It was revealed to the prophet Daniel that the meaning of the signs and timetables given to him some 2,500 years ago would be closed up and "sealed" until the time of the end (Daniel 12:9). If we are as close to the end of the age as many agree, and if the Almighty Creator has, indeed, now chosen to "unseal" and to reveal His "appointed times" to those who seek Him, it would not at all surprise me that He would pick out a servant like Randy Bullock to be His vessel.

James Bramlett.
Orlando, Florida

Contents

Contents (continued)

Publisher's Note

Why are we convinced that this is the generation which will witness the return of the Lord Jesus Christ? Is His return so imminent?

In Luke's gospel, chapter 21 verse 28 it is recorded that Jesus said *"And when these things begin to come to pass, then look up, and lift up your heads; for your redemption draweth nigh."* A close examination of this, and other related prophecies clearly indicate that **all those things have begun to come to pass** - technologically, politically, spiritually and physically.

Having studied Biblical time cycles and patterns, together with numerics and their significance, during the last four years I am convinced that there are many evidences hidden within the Word of God which give clear understanding of the timing of all the major prophetic events that are yet to be fulfilled. I have received constant confirmations in a number of ways that this is what the Lord desires to reveal to His people in these end times.

I believe that one of the confirmations is the fact that individuals living in all corners of the world, including such places as New Zealand, Australia, Africa, America, Canada, Holland, Finland and the United Kingdom have, for some years, been moved by the Holy Spirit to search the Word of God in a new light concerning such things as the timing of the rapture, the Tribulation, Daniel's 70th week, the Lord's return and His millennial reign. The results are quite startling; the more so when it is realised that although each of these people approach the work from different angles their findings are so very close.

It was as a result of a letter I wrote to Steve Terrell the author of *"The 90's: Decade of the Apocalypse"* that I contacted Randy Bullock who sent me his original work in the form of a paper. When I read it I was greatly encouraged and felt that his work should be made available for further research and consideration.

I am not so much concerned whether or not Randy's actual dates are correct as I am about the reality that faces us all - **the Lord's return is imminent** - within a short time the curtain will come down on the age of grace, which will then herald in a time of terrible world-wide tribulation to be followed by the judgment of the nations and then the long-awaited establishment of the everlasting kingdom of the King of Kings and Lord of Lords, the Lord Jesus Christ. My friend, will *"that day"* overtake you as a thief in the night? - I hope not.

My prayer is that this book will encourage you to earnestly **seek the Lord** concerning the days in which we live, that each and every day you will make Him **your priority,** and **that you will "look up"** - in the knowledge that your redemption does indeed draw very nigh!

Preface

Few Christians will probably ever see this paper, and no doubt even fewer will take the time and effort it would require to understand it. I have no illusions this paper will change many minds, for I am well aware of the resistance to any such work as this. It would be my first choice to not distribute this work outside my own small circle of family and friends; however, I feel an obligation to share it with others, so I have decided to weather whatever repercussions might ensue. There is, I want to emphasize, absolutely no profit motive on my part. I will not take any money for copies of this paper, and all who would want one may write to me for a free copy.

2 Peter 1:20 teaches us "No prophecy of Scripture is a matter of one's own interpretation." The meaning behind this admonition is that Scripture means only that which God intends it to mean. Scripture is not dependent upon our interpretations, rather it speaks for itself. These timetables, therefore, are a correct interpretation if, and only if, they contain the meaning God intended.

If any would have comments or suggestions, I can be reached at: P.O. Box 522, Danville, Illinois, 61834.

Maranatha

Randy Bullock

First printing: 29th June 1995
Second printing: 3rd June 1996
Third printing: 20th November 1996

The Appointed Times
Introduction

Our Bible tells us over and over again that Jesus of Nazareth will one day return to this earth. One example of this clear doctrine is:

John 14:2-3 (N.A.S.) *"In my Father's house are many dwelling places; if it were not so, I would have told you; for I go to prepare a place for you. And if I go and prepare a place for you, I will come again, and receive you to Myself; that where I am, there you may be also."*

For nearly 2,000 years the church has believed that Jesus will return. As Marvin Rosenthal has said, "Jesus is coming again. That fact is an inviolable absolute, an immutable certainty". (p115) The world, of course, usually scoffs at us. We have waited so long, and to those who do not share our faith, our hope is mere foolishness. To the world, we are like a bride that has been left at the altar, waiting for a groom that will never arrive. And yet we wait. And we do believe. Central to our faith is the conviction that our Lord will one day return.

The purpose of this paper is to ask and answer the question, "When will Christ return?" Many Christians will immediately object to this question even being asked. Most Christian end-time scholars have adamantly maintained that we cannot know the timing of the Parousia. They claim several Bible passages dispose of the matter, and that to even ask the question is, in effect, to disregard clear teaching from Scripture. The passages they cite are:

Matthew 24:42: *" Therefore be on the alert, for you do not know which day your Lord is coming."*

Matthew 24:36: *"But of that day and hour no one knows, not even the angels of heaven, nor the Son, but the Father alone."* See also Mark 13:32; Matthew 25:13.

Acts 1:6-7: *"And so when they had come together, they were* *asking Him, saying, 'Lord, is it at this time You are restoring the kingdom to Israel?' He said to them, 'It is not for you to know times or epochs which the Father has fixed by His own authority';"*

These verses, taken only by themselves, would indeed make a strong argument that we cannot know the exact day and hour that Jesus will return. Like so many other verses, however, they must be read in concert with the rest of Scripture and they must be read carefully. It is my belief the above Scriptures have been misunderstood and made to say more than they actually mean. I believe we can know when our Lord will return, and I base that belief on the following:

1. The verses cited above are not 'all-inclusive, universal statements'. All Scripture is written for all people, but this does not mean each verse must apply to each believer in exactly the same way. Christ made some statements meant to be directly applied to only His immediate listeners. Matthew 16:20 is a good example:

"Then he warned the disciples that they should tell no one that He was the Christ."

There is no reason to demand Matthew 24:36 is a universal statement. It is a statement Christ made to His disciples and it has time value. It is a statement that tells us the disciples did not know the timing of the Lord's return, but it is not a statement that demands subsequent believers will not or cannot know when He will return. Note Jesus did not say, "No one will ever know the day or the hour". All He said was "No one knows." Jesus was telling us that at the time He made the statement no one, except the Father, knew when He would return. Notice the passage tells us even Jesus himself did not know the day and hour of His return. If Christ's statement was meant to be a universal statement which demands no one can ever know the timing of His return, then we must conclude that even now Jesus does not know when He is coming back. Christ is now One with the Father, and surely knows all that the Father knows. To believe Christ does not know the day and hour of His return, while God the Father does, is to deny

4

the Oneness of the Trinity. If, instead, Christ does now know the day and the hour, then His statement in Matthew 24:36 must have been a statement that has time value and was directed at the listeners in His immediate audience.

2.   At least two Bible verses seem to hint that the Bible might contain information about the timing of end-time events:

Amos 3:7: *"Surely the Lord God does nothing Unless He reveals His secret counsel To His servants the prophets."*

Luke 8:17: *"For nothing is hidden that shall not become evident, nor anything secret that shall not be known and come to light."* See also Luke 12:2; Matthew 10:26; Mark 4:22.

3.   When Jesus came the first time, there was a small minority, including the wise men from the east (Matthew 2:1-12) and Simeon (Luke 2:21-38), who knew they were in the day of the First Advent.

4.   In Thessalonians 5:2-6 it is stated very clearly that believers should be watching for our Lord's return. It is not the Lord's intent for His return to be a surprise to those who are alert and watching for Him:

1 Thessalonians 5:2-6: *"For you yourselves know full well that the day of the Lord will come just like a thief in the night. While they are saying, 'Peace and safety!' then sudden destruction will come upon them suddenly like birth pangs upon a woman with child; and they shall not escape. But you, brethren, are not in darkness, that the day should overtake you like a thief; for you are all sons of light and sons of day. We are not of night nor of darkness; so then let us not sleep as others do, but let us be alert and sober."*

5.   All of the prophets seem to have been very interested in the question of when the promised Messiah would arrive. I believe

5

Daniel was especially concerned about the matter, and a close reading of his book reveals it is a major underlying theme of his writings. In chapter 12 a heavenly being asks the question, "How long will it be until the end of these wonders?" the 'man dressed in linen' (surely Christ) gave him an answer that was in the form of a riddle - a riddle that I believe has never before been solved. When Daniel heard the riddle, he did not understand it, and when he tried to get more information he was told:

> **Daniel 12:9-10:** *"..... 'Go your way Daniel, for these words are concealed and sealed up until the end time. Many will be purged, purified and refined; but the wicked will act wickedly, and none of the wicked will understand, but those who have insight will understand'."*

"Those who have insight will understand." Read Daniel 12 closely in concert with reading this paper and I believe you will agree that the question which those with insight will understand is the question posed by the angelic being in verse 6. That question is: *"How long will it be until the end of these wonders?"* In effect this question is: When will our Lord return? The prophets before Daniel longed to know when the Messiah would come, and Daniel was given the answer but he could not understand it. Even Christ's disciples were told they were not to know. However, at the time of the end, we are told in Daniel there will be those who understand.

The premise of this paper is that the book of Daniel contains three timetables. Each timetable is given to us as a separate riddle, and each, when solved, points to the exact same day for the Second Advent. The timetables also reveal several other dates, including the date the Antichrist covenant will be made and the date when believers will be raptured.

Daniel's First Timetable
The Ram and the Goat

Daniel's first timetable was given to him when he was approximately 67 years old, some 13 years before he received the second one. This timetable is preserved for us, embedded within the 8th chapter of Daniel. Daniel chapter 8 is a remarkable chapter in many ways. It is a passage filled with intrigue and mystery and one cannot read it without realizing he has been witness to a very important message from God. Scholars have dissected this chapter word-by-word, and yet the only real consensus about it is that it is very difficult. Not only is the Hebrew very difficult to translate, the message itself seems beyond comprehension. This paper will present a new way to look at the end-time message contained in this chapter.

Daniel begins the chapter with an account of a vision about a ram and a goat. Classical conservative understanding of this vision teaches us the ram represents Medo-Persia, and the goat, Greece. This interpretation, on one level, is clearly a correct one; however, the chapter can be fully understood only if one realizes it is prophecy that will have a dual fulfilment. Numerous scholars correctly understand the first fulfilment which took place during the era of Alexander the Great, and even the more liberal ones are amazed at how precisely it unfolded. The passage itself clearly leads us to understand this first fulfilment, since at verses 20 and 21 we are told the ram represents the Kings of Media and Persia, and the shaggy goat represents the kingdom of Greece. There are many great scholarly works that chronicle how this passage mirrors a piece of known history. Some scholars write that this portion of Daniel is the very best example of detailed prophecy that has been fulfilled by history. The Bible, however, clearly tells us this understanding of the prophecy is **an** understanding of it (verse 16) not **the** understanding of the vision. We are told three different times the vision also pertains to the *"time of the end"*:

Verse 17: *"..... understand that the vision pertains to the time of the end."*

7

Verse 19: *" ..... Behold, I am going to let you know what will occur at the final period of the indignation, for it pertains to the appointed time of the end."*

Verse 26: *"..... For it pertains to many days in the future."*

Many scholars agree this passage will have a dual fulfilment. John F. Walvoord, in his classic work, **"Daniel, The Key to Prophetic Revelation"**, points this out on page 192:

" ..... based upon the principle of dual fulfilment of prophecy, that Daniel 8 is intentionally a prophetic reference both to Antiochus Epiphanes, now fulfilled, and to the end of the age and the final world ruler who persecutes Israel before the second advent."

Walvoord, himself, subscribes to a slightly different theory that maintains the passage is "intentionally typical", meaning that the primary fulfilment was during the years of Alexander and Antiochus, but that much of the passage points to events that will occur at the end times. Walvoord's arguments for a dual fulfilment of this prophecy are very strong, while those scholars who have tried to maintain that Daniel 8 has no end-time significance have no convincing answer for why Gabriel would call the era of Alexander and Antiochus the *"appointed time of the end"*. It seems very clear to me this passage must have a fulfilment which will unfold in the last days, and it is my belief part of this latter-day fulfilment has recently taken place.

The first seven verses of the chapter prophesy, I believe, the recent war between the United States and Iraq. As remarkable as that conclusion may seem, I am convinced it is a correct one. The following is a verse by verse explanation of how I understand the fulfilment of these verses:

Verse 1. *"In the third year of the reign of Belshazzar the king a vision appeared to me, Daniel, subsequent to the one which appeared to me previously."*

Verse 2: *"and I looked in the vision, and it came about while I*

8

was looking, that I was in the citadel of Susa, which is in the province of Elam; and I looked in the vision, and I myself was beside the Ulai Canal."

Daniel was in the citadel of Susa (modern-day Iran) when he received this vision. The vision projects Daniel to the Ulai canal which is near Susa. Daniel saw a ram standing in front, that is, on the other side of the canal, which means that Daniel must have been looking in the direction of Babylon, modern-day Iraq.

Verse 3: *"Then I lifted my gaze and looked, and behold, a ram which had two horns was standing in front of the canal. Now the two horns were long, but one was longer than the other, with the longer one coming up last."*

The ram has two long horns, the longest of which comes up last. It is well known Bible symbolism that animals often represent kingdoms, and horns represent a country's military strength. The Bible is telling us this country will twice have a strong military and its most powerful army will be its second one. Note I am not saying the first horn is Medo-Persia and the second modern-day Iraq. The second fulfilment of this vision is separate from the first, and each detail in it relates only to the second fulfilment. The horns of the ram will both be shattered by the goat, which means, I believe, the United States will go back to Iraq and fight this battle a second time. Since the last horn of this ram is longer than the first, it must mean that Iraq's second army will be stronger than the first one the United States defeated. This may mean Iraq will have some nuclear weapons.

Verse 4: *"I saw the ram butting westward, northward, and southward, and no other beasts could stand before him, nor was there anyone to rescue from his power; but he did as he pleased and magnified himself."*

The ram is seen butting westward, northward and southward. To the west of Iraq is Israel, to the north, Turkey, and to the south is Kuwait and Saudi Arabia. The Iraqi invasion of Kuwait was the trigger that pulled the U.S. into the conflict; however, Saddam Hussein was also involved in a struggle with the Kurds to the north and the Jews to the west. Turkey and Saudi Arabia, both allowed the U.S. to use air bases during the war, and Israel had to be persuaded to not jump into the fighting. Just as the vision prophesies, Saddam Hussein butted west, north, and south, and when the U.S. entered into the picture, the countries from those directions helped us to butt back. Notice, however, that the ram was not seen butting eastward, toward Iran. Although Iraq fought a bitter 8 year war with Iran a few years prior to this conflict, during the time frame this vision pertains to, Iraq is not butting to the east. For all practical purposes, Iran remained neutral during the conflict.

The ram *"did as he pleased and magnified himself"*. The ram represents the country of Iraq; however, the personality described here is a clear depiction of her leader. Saddam Hussein is a dictator who has made it a practice to do as he pleases and he seldom misses an opportunity to magnify himself. His purpose in invading Kuwait was to capture the oil and riches that would further his goal to magnify himself.

> **Verse 5:** *"While I was observing, behold, a male goat was coming from the west over the surface of the whole earth without touching the ground; and the goat had a conspicuous horn between his eyes."*

Out of the west came a goat with a *"conspicuous horn between his eyes"*. The U.S. and her allies, of course, came from the west, and we came with a quite "conspicuous" horn. Several scholars remark in their commentaries about the Hebrew word, "chazuth" that is translated here as "conspicuous". The way the word is used in the sentence leads experts to believe that somehow the horn could see. Leupold, on page 340 calls it a *"horn of vision"* and Goldingay, on page 196, refers to it as *"a horn of visibility"*. It is also worth noting that no animal has its horn or horns between its eyes. Horns are usually located on the top or side of the animal's head, so that in order to attack it must put its head down and look at the ground. A bull, for instance, cannot clearly see what it is driving at, because its eyes are down when it charges. This goat, however, has its horn between its eyes and can therefore always see its target. Anyone who watched the U.S./Iraqi war on CNN will remember the great display that we put on with our so-called "smart bombs". Our bombs and missiles could literally see, and we were able to send them on precise missions that displayed an accuracy in warfare never before known to man. Not only could we hit individual buildings at will, but we could destroy hardened bunkers by sending our bombs down ventilation shafts! The horn of the U.S. and her allies could literally see. It was a horn of vision.

Even though the goat is pictured here as somewhat of a hero, others that are described elsewhere in the Bible as male goats are not always being complemented. The best illustration of this is in Ezekiel 34:17-20:

> *"And as for you, My flock, thus says the Lord God, 'Behold, I will judge between one sheep and another, between the rams and the male goats. Is it too slight a thing for you that you should feed in the good pasture, that you must tread down with your feet the rest of your pastures? Or that you should drink of the clear waters, that you must foul the rest with your feet? And as for My flock, they must eat what you tread down with your feet, and they must drink what you foul with your feet!' Therefore, thus says the Lord God to them, 'Behold, I, even I, will judge between the fat sheep and the lean sheep.'"*

Although we Americans are reluctant to look at ourselves as a selfish goat that spoils the pasture and clear waters, much of the world would describe us in such a way. We are less than 5% of the world's population, and yet we consume 25% of its resources. Though we pay for the resources we take, we none the less take far more than our share, and we often destroy and pollute as we do so.

Verse 5 says this male goat came *"from the west over the surface of the whole earth without touching the ground"*. Of all the details in this passage, this, to me, is the one that most clearly points to the recent conflict between the U.S. and Iraq. In interpreting this detail, as it relates to the first fulfilment of the vision, scholars remark that

Alexander had a very mobile army that was exceedingly swift for its day. If that interpretation is acceptable, and I believe it must be, then the U.S. forces fit the vision even better. Our forces **literally** crossed the **whole earth** without touching the ground. Hartman and Di Lella comment on page 224 that the Hebrew translated here as *"without (his) touching the ground"* literally means *"with no one touching the ground".* We travelled by air and by sea from one end of this earth to the other, and probably not one of our soldiers stepped his foot on the ground until the entire journey was made!

> **Verse 6:** *"And he came up to the ram that had the two horns, which I had seen standing in front of the canal, and rushed at him in his mighty wrath."*
>
> **Verse 7:** *"And I saw him come beside the ram, and he was enraged at him; and he struck the ram and shattered his two horns, and the ram had no strength to withstand him. So he hurled him to the ground and trampled on him, and there was none to rescue the ram from his power."*

The goat in the vision apparently did not come from the west and immediately charge the ram. Verse seven says he came up *"beside"* the ram and then he struck him. There seems to be some emphasis on the fact that although this was a fierce attack and full of rage, it was done with precision and deliberation. The U.S., of course, acted exactly that way. We landed in Saudi Arabia and prepared for over five months before we launched our invasion.

Note also, Daniel again mentions he had seen the ram *"in front of"* that is, on the other side of the canal. The Ulai Canal was in what is now modern-day Iran near the Iraqi border, and the "other side" of that canal is in the direction of Iraq. Canals and rivers often delineate borders, and the Bible elsewhere uses them in symbolic fashion when borders between powers or countries are being represented. The original dispute that created this conflict was over borders. Kuwait and Iraq had argued for years over the exact location of the borders between them. Iraq used the dispute for pretence to invade and take over its much smaller and weaker neighbour. This chapter at its core is about borders. It is about conflicts over borders, and who will rule whom. The theme is basic to understanding the passage as well as the four chapters that follow through the end of the book.

When the goat struck the ram we are told the goat *"rushed at him in his mighty wrath"* and the goat was *"enraged"*. We are told the ram was hurled to the ground and that the goat then trampled on him. This description quite aptly pictures the one-sided war that was fought. First, the Americans wiped out Iraq's air defense and then we trampled their ground forces. The U.S. lost approximately 300 troops, versus tens of thousands on the Iraqi side. *"And there was none to rescue the ram from his power."* Though a country or two verbally sided with Iraq, and King Hussein allowed her to use Jordan's supply routes, none attempted to help Iraq militarily and of course, none even tried to rescue her from the power of our great military might.

If the Bible really does contain prophecy that accurately predicts events that occur centuries after the prophet sees them, then we should sincerely consider whether this passage does indeed prophesy the recent war that the world so closely witnessed via live television coverage. Is there another conflict in all of history that better fits the vision? The answer, I strongly believe, is clearly "NO". Nearly all scholars, liberal and conservative alike, agree that the invasion of Medo-Persia by Alexander the Great is an extremely accurate fulfilment of this vision, and yet the second fulfilment, as I have attempted to describe above, is even more precise. One might think God could see 200 years into the future more clearly than 25 centuries, but here, I believe, is proof He sees all of the future in perfect detail.

These first seven verses of the second fulfilment of this chapter are all that have to-date occurred. The rest of the chapter is still future; however, I believe we can now substantially analyse what is yet to unfold. The following is a verse by verse attempt to understand the rest of this vision. Embedded in the middle of the following is what I call Daniel's first timetable. It will agree with the second and the third timetables which will be presented later.

Verse 8: *"Then the male goat magnified himself exceedingly.*

> *But as soon as he was mighty, the large horn was broken; and in*
> *its place there came up four conspicuous horns toward the four*
> *winds of heaven."*

Since our war with Iraq, the U.S. has indeed *"magnified itself greatly"*.
We are a nation proud of our wealth, our democracy, our capitalism,
and our accomplishments. Our national tone has become exceedingly
proud. We insist that democracy and capitalism are the best systems
to live under, and in fact we have often demanded that others follow
our lead. We point to our military power and great industrial might,
and offer it as proof that we are superior. The people of the world
consider us an arrogant nation, and an unbiased observer would surely
agree with them.

The phrase *"But as soon as he was mighty"* can better be translated
"at a precise point during the peak of his strength". Goldingay, on
page 197 claims the Hebrew is *"expressing an exact point of time"*. It
is apparent the translation *"as soon as he was mighty"* does not fit the
rest of the vision, since the goat is certainly already very mighty when
he tramples the ram. The thought being conveyed is that the goat's
horn will be broken very suddenly at an exact point in time, and it will
be broken while the goat is at the peak of his power. The nation
represented by this goat will suddenly be broken, almost
instantaneously, like the snapping of an animal's horn. I believe this
verse is one of the numerous ones that prophesy the imminent
destruction of our beloved country.

In place of the goat's horn there will arise *"four conspicuous horns*
toward the four winds of heaven". When interpreting the first
fulfilment of this vision, scholars point out that when Alexander died
he was replaced by his four generals. The power that led the world, at
least for a while, continued to be the Grecian empire; however, it was
splintered into four distinct divisions. The destruction of the United
States will be so total, however, that this prophecy cannot be predicting
a similar fate for her. Instead, I believe, we are being told here the
leadership of the world will transfer to four other spheres. I expect
these spheres to be Russia and her allies, Europe, the Far East and the
Moslem nations. Just as was the case with the Greek Empire after

Alexander's death, the dominant world power will be transferred to four separate entities. Each of these spheres of power will point their horns *"towards the four winds of heaven"*.

The four winds of heaven are mentioned several times in Scripture, and they represent the messengers or the power that God sends to accomplish His purpose. When an animal points his horns towards another, it is an aggressive gesture that indicates hostility and a readiness to fight. The leading countries of the world will, in effect, "shake their fists" at God. They will not be in subjection but will rebel against the God of Heaven. Notice, however, the futility that is pictured here - a beast thrusting his horns at the wind! Regardless of the strength of the beast, it could never subdue the wind. The image drawn here reminds me of Psalms 2:1-4 and Psalms 59:5-9:

> *"Why are the nations in an uproar,*
> *And the peoples devising a vain thing?*
> *The kings of the earth take their stand,*
> *And the rulers take counsel together*
> *Against the Lord and against His Anointed:*
> *'Let us tear their fetters apart,*
> *And cast away their cords from us!'*
> *He who sits in the heavens laughs,*
> *The Lord scoffs at them."*   **Psalms 2:1-4**

> *"And Thou, O Lord God of hosts, the God of Israel,*
> *Awake to punish all the nations;*
> *Do not be gracious to any who are treacherous in iniquity.*
> *They return at evening, they howl like a dog,*
> *And go around the city.*
> *Behold, they belch forth with their mouth;*
> *Swords are in their lips,*
> *For, they say, 'Who hears?'*
> *But Thou, O Lord, dost laugh at them;*
> *Thou dost scoff at all the nations.*
> *Because of his strength I will watch for Thee,*
> *For God is my stronghold."*   **Psalms 59:5-9**

15

The Little Horn

The nations of the world, with all their power, are no match for the One who created the heavens and the earth. Continuing on with the eighth chapter of Daniel, verse 9 introduces the "small horn" that most pretribulation scholars believe represents the coming antichrist.

> **Verse 9:** *"And out of one of them came forth a rather small horn which grew exceedingly great toward the south, toward the east, and toward the Beautiful Land."*

Out of one of these spheres of power will arise a rather small horn. Notice there appears to be a bit of a switch in symbolism. The horns of this passage have represented the military power of the animal kingdoms, while now the "small horn" represents a man, the antichrist. The Bible elsewhere uses horns to represent kings, especially "warrior kings" that are aggressive militarily. Although the antichrist will start out small, he will grow *"exceedingly great toward the south, toward the east and toward the Beautiful Land"*. Nearly all scholars accept that the *"Beautiful Land"* represents Israel. The growing of this little horn toward these two directions and Israel probably indicates aggression, just as is the case of the thrusting horns in the previous verse and the growing horn of verse 10. This verse also appears to narrow down from what direction the antichrist will come. Since the antichrist attacks Israel, and he also attacks to the south and east, this verse seems to indicate that Israel will be either to the north or west of the country from where the antichrist comes. If Israel was either south or east of this horn, then the verse would be redundant, and it is probably correct to assume otherwise.

> **Verse 10:** *And it grew up to the host of heaven and caused some of the host and some of the stars to fall to the earth, and it trampled them down."*

The antichrist will attack *"the host of heaven"* and cause some of them and some of the *"stars to fall."* Many scholars believe the *"host"* represents the Jews and I believe the *"stars"* represent Christians.

There is no question that God's people, Jews and Christians alike, will be hated and trampled upon by the coming antichrist. A number of Bible passages, such as Daniel 7:25, Revelation 13:7, Revelation 11:7 and Daniel 8:24, make it abundantly clear a great persecution of Jews and Christians will accompany the great tribulation. While God is waging a spiritual war, using spiritual weapons (2 Corinthians 6:3-10; 2 Corinthians 10:4; Ephesians 6:10-18), Satan will be waging a war of the flesh. Some Christians, or maybe all Christians, will be raptured before the great tribulation, in order that we be saved *"from the wrath to come"* (1 Thessalonians 1:10 and Revelation 3:10). However, there will be conversions during the tribulation (Revelation 7:14), and those believers will be persecuted (Revelation 20:4).

Verse 11: *"It even magnified itself to be equal with the Commander of the host; and it removed the regular sacrifice from Him, and the place of His sanctuary was thrown down."*

The little horn, the antichrist, will even magnify itself to be equal with *"the commander of the host"*. The Commander of the host is, of course, God. The antichrist will declare himself to be God (2 Thessalonians 2:4), exalt himself, speak monstrous things against God (Daniel 11:36), and oppose Christ (Daniel 8:25).

The Transgression

The antichrist will also remove the regular sacrifice and throw down the sanctuary. Most pretribulation scholars expect the Jerusalem temple to be rebuilt and the daily sacrifices reinstated. Verse 11 tells us the antichrist will somehow throw down the temple and thereby put a stop to these ritual sacrifices. Daniel 9:27 and 11:31 apparently give us more information about this event. Many scholars hold that the antichrist will be in firm military control of the world by this time, and he will end the temple sacrifices by simple decree; however, when the several verses are read together, it seems apparent force is used. As Daniel 11:31 explains, *"forces from him will arise, desecrate the sanctuary fortress, and do away with the regular sacrifice"*.

> **Verse 12:** *"And on account of transgression the host will be given over to the horn along with the regular sacrifice; and it will fling truth to the ground and perform its will and prosper."*

This verse is an important one to read very closely. It says *"on account of transgression the host will be given over to the horn"*. Most scholars read this to say, in effect, a transgression will occur when the host, God's people, are given over to the horn. In other words, the antichrist will kill Jews and Christians, and when this happens it will be a transgression or sin. Notice, however, the army of God is given over to the antichrist *"on account of"*, or because of, a transgression. In other words, there will be a particular sin or transgression, and that sin will cause God's army to be persecuted. Note in verse 13 a definite article is placed before "transgression". It is called "the" transgression, not "a" transgression. This use of the definite article is also clear in the Hebrew text. It will not be sin in general that causes the persecution, but rather a particular sin - a specific transgression.

The question must now be asked, "what particular sin is committed, and who commits it?" Numerous commentators I have read attribute this transgression to the acts of the antichrist. I believe however, they have focused on the wrong sinner. I believe the particular sin committed is an attempted assassination of the antichrist, and *"on account of"* this assassination attempt the antichrist will strike out with great vengeance against all of God's army. It is possible that sincere believers misread Scripture and attempt to kill him or it might be that wolves in sheep's clothing do it. It may be that Jews attempt to kill him because of the desecration done to the temple (Daniel 11:31) and that both Jews and Christians suffer the consequences. Jeremiah 51:23 may indicate Jews cause the shattering of the flock. Whichever is the case, God's army is blamed and the slaughter will be a horrible one.

Several passages in Scripture tell us about this attempted assassination. Revelation 13:3 is the key:

> *"And I saw one of his heads as if it had been slain, and his fatal wound was healed. And the whole earth was amazed and followed after the beast;"*

Numerous scholars correctly understand it is the antichrist who has suffered this fatal wound. Most of them incorrectly conclude he will suffer a head wound because this verse says John saw *"one of his heads as if it had been slain"*. One cannot conclude, though, that the wound is a head wound. The beast of Revelation 13 has seven heads, each of which represents a king or leader, and one of those kings or leaders has been slain. What kind of fatal wound or apparently fatal wound the leader suffers, however, is not known from this text. We only know that verse 3 and verse 12 both call it a *"fatal wound"*. The *"head"* that is wounded is the antichrist himself; it is not necessary to conclude it is the antichrist's head that suffers the wound.

There are other passages in the Bible which give us additional information about this wound. We know from Revelation 13:14 that it is a sword wound. Many commentators claim this description can be taken idiomatically and it could be another kind of weapon is used. However, I prefer to take this verse literally. I believe the antichrist will suffer an actual sword or long knife wound. Another possible reference to this wound is given in:

Habakkuk 3:13.
"Thou didst go forth for the salvation of Thy people,
For the salvation of Thine anointed.
Thou didst strike the head of the house of the evil
To lay him open from thigh to neck."

If this passage does refer to the attempted assassination of the antichrist, then he will be cut open from his thigh to his neck. Translators are not sure if Habakkuk 3:13 says *"thigh to neck,"* or *"foundation to the neck".* so the exact nature of the wound is not precisely known. Apparently, though, it is a very extensive sword wound. It is also possible that the antichrist's heart will be cut out (Daniel 4:16) and that he will be given an animal's heart (Daniel 7:4). The N.A.S. version translates the Aramaic word *"lebab"* (Strongs #3825) as *"mind"*; however, it literally means *"heart".* The King James and the Interlinear Bible (literal translation) both render lebab as *"heart"* in both Daniel 4:16 and 7:4. There may be a head wound too (Habakkuk 3:14). Consider also Genesis 3:15; Psalms 68:21; Psalms 74:14 and Isaiah 27:1.

Habakkuk relays to us in verse 16 what happens after the *"head of the house of evil"* is cut *"open from thigh to neck"*:

"I heard and my inward parts trembled,
At the sound my lips quivered.
Decay enters my bones,
And in my place I tremble.
Because I must wait quietly for the day of distress,
For the people to arise who will invade us."

Habakkuk's inward parts trembled and his lips quivered, because *"I must wait quietly for the day of distress, for the people to arise who will invade us".* Habakkuk's reaction was very similar to Daniel's. The vision of God's army being slaughtered was very disturbing to Daniel, too. Daniel 8:27 tells us that the vision left him *"exhausted and sick for days".*

Continuing on with verse 12 of Daniel 8, we are told the antichrist

21

will *"fling truth to the ground and perform its will and prosper"*. A number of Bible passages make it abundantly clear the antichrist will appear to be winning his war against God. If accomplishments of the flesh are what ultimately matter, then the antichrist will be very successful indeed. He will be a great leader who will *"mislead, if possible, even the elect"* (Matthew 24:24), and he will be worshipped by *"all who dwell on the earth"* (Revelation 13:8).

> **Verse 13:** *"Then I heard a holy one speaking, and another holy one said to that particular one who was speaking, 'How long will the vision about the regular sacrifice apply, while the transgression causes horror, so as to allow both the holy place and the host to be trampled'?"*

This verse presents to us a question that will be answered in verse 14. The answer will be in the form of a riddle that when properly solved provides the basis of Daniel's first timetable. In order to understand the answer, however, it is necessary to first understand the question. Scholars admit they are not sure how the question should be translated and consequently they are not even sure what question is being asked. Walvoord calls the Hebrew "very difficult".

The holy one who asks the question is narrowing in on the part of the vision that prophesies the trampling of the holy place and the host. He is wanting to know how long the horror will last. Notice also his question contains information. We are told the transgression *"causes"* the horror, and the transgression *"allows"* the holy place and the host to be trampled. We know this already from verse 12 where we are told the host is given over to the horn *"on account"* of the transgression; however the wording of the holy one's question makes this point even more clear. The question the holy one is asking, then, can be broken down into a brief statement and a question that could be worded as follows:

> *"The vision informs us about the removal of the regular sacrifice and about the transgression that causes the holy place and the host to be trampled. How long will this horror against the holy place and the host last?"*

The holy one is linking the removal of the regular sacrifice to the transgression, so it is possible that the attempted assassination is carried out as revenge for the desecration of the sanctuary (Daniel 11:31). The sequence of events, then, is as follows:

Forces from the antichrist desecrate the sanctuary and do away with the regular sacrifice;

Someone then attempts to assassinate the antichrist, and the antichrist blames Jews and Christians;

The antichrist then seeks revenge and carries out a horrible trampling of God's people.

The question the holy one is asking, therefore, is

"How long will this horrible trampling last?"

The trampling will begin the moment the assassination is attempted, since Habakkuk 3:14 indicates the perpetrators of the transgression are stormed by the antichrist's guards. The New International Version translates Habakkuk 3:14 differently than does the N.A.S. or other popular translations. The N.I.V. indicates the antichrist is pierced with his own spear and his warriors will then storm in to defend him. The N.I.V. reads:

"With his own spear you pierced his head when his warriors stormed out to scatter us, ..."

Therefore, the question being asked at Daniel 8:13 is:

"How long will it be from the committing of the transgression until the horror stops?"

The answer to that question is given in verse 14.

2,300 Evenings and Mornings

Daniel Chapter 8 verse 14: *"And he said to me, 'For 2,300 evenings and mornings; then the holy place will be properly restored'."*

The answer to the question *"how long will this horrible trampling last?"* is *"2,300 evenings and mornings"*. In English, we have the expression "day and night" which we use when we want to emphasize something is constant and continual. One might, for instance, describe a painful injury by saying "I suffered day and night for over three weeks." I believe the holy one's answer is emphasizing the constant and continual nature of the persecution. The persecution will be unrelenting, and it will last for 2,300 nights and days.

Scholars have debated this verse at very great length. Many have tried to understand it and solve the riddle by attributing the 2,300 evenings and mornings to various time spans in the past. Jerusalem has, of course, been trampled several times before, and a number of scholars have seen those events as the fulfilment of this prophecy. Many conservative scholars, however, especially those who are pretribulationists, believe the prophecy may have had a typical fulfilment in the past but its primary fulfilment will be during the great tribulation which is yet future. Some have concluded that 2,300 evenings and mornings are equal to 2,300 full days, but their arguments seem influenced by a desire to find a time span that approximates the 7 year great tribulation. Carl Friedrich Keil in his book **"Biblical Commentary on the Book of Daniel,"** considers the matter at considerable length and concludes the 2,300 evenings and mornings "must" be 2,300 full days. Many other scholars have followed Keil's lead and are just as adamant. However, it is simply not correct to conclude Keil's work disposes the matter.

Many other scholars are on the other side of this issue and are just as convinced that Keil is wrong. Gleason L. Archer Jr., for instance, states on page 103 of **"The Expositor's Bible Commentary"** that "both views have persuasive advocates, but the preponderance of evidence seems to favour the latter interpretation." Those scholars, such as Archer, that maintain the 2,300 evenings and mornings are 1,150 evenings and 1,150 mornings have, in my opinion, by far the best case. Although *"2,300 evenings and mornings"* is a difficult expression, Scripture gives us several other verses which we can use to help us understand it. Four times the Bible uses the expression *"forty days and forty nights"* (Genesis 7:4 and 12; Exodus 24:18; 1 Kings 19:8; Matt 4:2), and each time it is referring to 40 twenty-four hour days. The flood rains fell for 40 days, Moses spent 40 days on Mount Sinai, Elijah journeyed for 40 days and Jesus fasted for 40 full days.. Each of these passages repeat the number 40 in order to convey the meaning of 40 full days. Notice however, that in Daniel 8:14 the number "2300" is not repeated, and therefore does not refer to 2300 full days.Forty days and forty nights is the expression used to mean 40 full days and never does the Bible say 40 days and nights as a way to express 40 full days. The same argument holds for the expression 3 days and 3 nights (Jonah 1:17; Matthew 12:40). Just as "40 dogs and cats" does not mean the same as "40 dogs and 40 cats," so also *"2,300 evenings and mornings"* surely does not mean the same as does "2,300 evenings and 2,300 mornings."

After the 2,300 evenings and mornings pass, *"then the holy place will be properly restored"*. The N.A.S. translates the Hebrew word used here "tsadeq" (Strongs #6663), as *"restored."* Many experts, however, believe it should be translated *"vindicated"* or *"justified"*. I believe *"vindicated"* best conveys the meaning that is meant here. After the 2,300 evenings and mornings then the holy place will be properly "vindicated". Note also 2,300 evenings and mornings is a span that will cover 1,151 of our standard days. If the horror starts the evening or night of the attempted assassination, it will end the day of the 1,151st day following.

The horrible trampling shall begin, therefore, when an attempt is made to assassinate the antichrist, and it will end when the holy place, or Israel, is vindicated. We must now address the issue of what is meant by the "vindication" of Israel.

26

The Day of the Lord

The final and ultimate vindication of Israel will take place, I believe, on the great Day of the Lord. The Bible has much to say about a Day of the Lord which will one day befall this earth. Prophecy about the Day of the Lord is often interwoven with prophecy that covers a broader time span, and therefore many commentators consider the entire seven year tribulation to be the Day of the Lord. Some pretribulationists even consider the entire thousand year millennium as part of what the Bible calls *"the Day of the Lord"*. I believe, however, it will literally be a single day that refers to the hours just before Christ's return as King. The *"Day of the Lord"* is the Hebrew day on which our Lord will come back. This paper's conclusion will be that Christ will return as King sometime during the daylight hours (daytime in Israel) of May 14th 2004. Since the Hebrew day starts at sunset and ends at sunset, the Day of the Lord will begin the night of May 13th and end the day of May 14th 2004. The following selected verses are offered in an attempt to outline what I believe the Bible means by the great Day of the Lord:

Psalms 79:6-7:
"Pour out Thy wrath upon the nations which do not know Thee,
And upon the kingdoms which do not call upon Thy name.
For they have devoured Jacob,
And laid waste his habitation."

Isaiah 10:17:
"And the light of Israel will become a fire
and his Holy One a flame,
And it will burn and devour his thorns and
his briars in a single day."

Joel 1:15:
"Alas for the day!
For the day of the Lord is near,
And it will come as destruction from the Almighty."

Joel 2:1-2:
"Blow the trumpet in Zion,

27

And sound an alarm on My holy mountain!
Let all the inhabitants of the land tremble,
For the day of the Lord is coming;
Surely it is near,
A day of darkness and gloom,
A day of clouds and thick darkness."

Zephaniah 1:14-16:
"Near is the great day of the Lord,
Near and coming very quickly;
Listen, the day of the Lord!
In it the warrior cries out bitterly.
A day of wrath is that day,
A day of trouble and distress,
A day of destruction and desolation,
A day of darkness and gloom,
A day of clouds and thick darkness,
A day of trumpet and battle cry,
Against the fortified cities
And the high corner towers."

The Hebrew word *"ereb"* translated in Daniel 8:14 as *"evening"* refers to the hours between sunset and sunrise. It means, for our purposes here, the same as what we mean by *"night-time"*. The Hebrew word *"boqer"* translated here as *"morning"* refers to the hours between sunrise and sunset. For out purposes, boqer means the same as our *"daytime"*. The Jewish day starts at sunset and ends at sunset the next day, so their day does not coincide perfectly with ours. Our day begins in the middle of the night, which if one thinks about it, seems a bit odd, while the Jewish day is a reflection of Genesis 1:5. It is important for us to realize a Jewish "evening" is all of the hours of darkness, and therefore encompasses part of two of our days, while the Jewish "morning" is all the daylight hours and is contained within only one of our days. The point that needs to be made is the "evening" of March 20th 2001 will encompass the last 6 hours or so of March 20th and approximately the first six hours of March 21st.

Attempted Assassination

This paper will offer three separate avenues that will lead to the conclusion that Jesus will return as King on May 14th 2004. At this point, however, we will have to assume that date in order to calculate the date when the attempted assassination of the antichrist will occur. If we know Jesus will return on May 14th, 2004, we can calculate backwards and find the attempted assassination of the antichrist will take place during the evening of March 20th or the first 6 hours of March 21st, 2001, which is precisely 2,300 evenings and mornings or "nights and days" before the evening or "night" or May 13th 2004. I believe someone will attempt to kill the antichrist sometime between sunset and dawn during the night of March 20th. Note, however, the Jewish evening or night of March 20th also includes the first 6 hours or so of March 21st.

When I calculated backwards to arrive at the March 20th, March 21st date, the date seemed to be a familiar one. I knew it marked some kind of observance, but was not at all sure what. With just a little bit of research, I discovered that spring equinox always occurs, depending upon the year, on either March 20th or 21st. The equinox is that time of year (once in the spring and once in the fall) when the day and night are of near equal length everywhere on earth. It is quite interesting that the Bible calls this chapter of Daniel the *"Vision of the Evening and Morning"* (verse 26), which most commentators believe is a reference to the evening and morning sacrifices to which the antichrist puts a stop. "Evening" and "morning" are both singular, however, so this phrase must refer to a particular evening and morning rather than the 2,300 given in verse 14. Note that although the N.A.S. and other versions pluralize both "Evening" and "Morning," apparently to synchronize with verse 14, the Hebrew manuscripts clearly show both as singular. The spring equinox of 2001 will be at approximately 4.32pm Jerusalem time, March 20th, which means the length of the day of March 20th will be a near perfect match with the length of the night which follows.

Gabriel may have named this vision *"The Vision of the Evening and*

Morning" because the entire vision pivots around the transgression which will occur during the night of the spring equinox.

It is curious the date calculated for the occurrence of the transgression happens to be the night of the spring equinox. The coincidence, however, does not stop here. March 21st is also the first day of the Ides of March. The Ides of March is usually considered the 15th day of the month; however, in its broader sense, it also includes the 7 days preceding the 15th. In the Old Roman calendar, the Ides of March was the 8th through 15th of March. The Old Roman calendar is the Julian calendar and it currently lags our modern calendar by 13 days. The Ides of March, for the year 2001, according to the Old Roman calendar, will be March 21st through the 28th. The great Roman general and dictator, Julius Caesar, was also assassinated during the Ides of March. He was stabbed to death by aristocratic enemies that had pretended to be his friends.

My analysis leads me to believe that whoever attempts to assassinate the antichrist will choose the March 21st timing, because it is the first day of the Ides of March, a day that will carry heavy and obvious symbolism for them.

Summary of Daniel 8:12-14

The foregoing analysis is what I consider to be the correct interpretation of Daniel 8:12-14. The following is a summary of that analysis:

1. A transgression or sin will cause God's people to be trampled by the antichrist.

2. The transgression that will occur is the attempted assassination of the antichrist.

3. The trampling is called a "horror" and it is very upsetting to Daniel and the holy ones who are being told about it. One of the holy ones asks a question which can be worded as *"How long will this horrible trampling last?"*

4. The answer to the question is the trampling will begin when the transgression occurs and will end 2,300 nights and days later when the holy place, Jerusalem, is vindicated.

5. Jerusalem will be vindicated on the Day of the Lord, which will begin at sunset on May 13th, 2004 and end sometime the following day when Jesus returns as King.

6. The attempted assassination will take place in the early morning hours before dawn on March 21st, 2001. Counting inclusively from the night of March 20-21st through the day of May 13th, 2004, there are precisely 2,300 nights and days or *"evenings and mornings"*.

7. The night of March 20-21st is the night of the spring equinox of that year and thus Gabriel titles the entire vision the *"Vision of the Evening and Morning"*. March 21st will also be the first day of the Ides of March and, therefore, the reason the antichrist's assassins choose that date to commit their crime.

Notice I believe an assassination attempt, even on the coming antichrist, is a sin. I believe the Bible is calling this act a transgression or a sin. Although it is prophesied in several Biblical passages, it is not an act God is authorizing or condoning. Daniel 8:25 tells us the antichrist will be broken *"without human agency"*, or as the literal reads, *"without a hand"*. The Bible tells us over and over God's army will prevail by the word of God. We are told, for instance, in Revelation 19:15 Christ's sword is not made of metal; it is instead a spiritual sword made of His Word. We are told in 2 Corinthians 10:4 *"the weapons of our warfare are not of the flesh, but divinely powerful for the destruction of fortresses"*. Our weapons are not the weapons the world uses, instead they are the weapons of righteousness, patience, kindness, and genuine love. Our armour is truth, peace and faith.

Antichrist's Solution to the Riddle

There is also what I consider to be an incorrect solution to the riddle given in Daniel 8:13-14. The antichrist will, I believe, consider himself to be the one who restores the holy place. When he makes the so-called "peace treaty" (Daniel 9:27), he will point to that date as the date the holy place is restored. He will twist the riddle to point to himself as part of his plan to declare himself God. In 2 Thessalonians 2:4 we are told *"he takes his seat in the temple of God, displaying himself as being God."* If the antichrist can interpret this passage in Daniel as a prophecy that points to himself, it would help him convince many that he is the Messiah the world has been waiting for. The following analysis outlines the false interpretation I believe he will use.

On previous pages, I have explained how the first 7 verses of this chapter prophesy the war our county had with Iraq. This war is depicted as a *"trampling"* (Daniel 8:7). The U.S. trampled Iraq, and in retribution Iraq and her allies have taken vengeance upon Israel. During the war, Iraq hit Israel with several scud missiles, and since then there have been a series of terrorist attacks launched against her.

The question the holy one asks in verse 13 could be wrongly understood to be a query about how long a stretch of time ensues between the trampling depicted in verse 7 and the restoration of the holy place prophesied in verse 14. In other words, the riddle could be understood to be prophesying how much time will elapse between the start of the U.S. war with Iraq and the signing of the antichrist covenant.

If the 2,300 "evenings and mornings" are understood, as many scholars contend, to be 2,300 full days, then the false interpretation of the riddle would predict that the antichrist will make the covenant with Israel 2,300 days after the start of the war. The U.S. attacked the Iraqi positions in the early morning hours of January 17th 1991, and 2,300 days from that date will be Sunday, May 4th 1997. That date happens to be Yom ha-Shoah which is the day Israel sets aside to remember the Holocaust. When the antichrist makes, or signs, the covenant with

33

Israel, he will no doubt be hailed as a peacemaker and a hero. To the Jewish people, the covenant they make with him will be an attempt to end the persecutions they have endured for so many centuries. It seems very logical they would choose Yom-ha-Shoah as the date to sign such an historic treaty. The word holocaust means "a sacrifice consumed by fire". If the so-called "peace treaty" is signed on Yom ha-Shoah, "The Day of Holocaust" then the human intent will no doubt be to emphasize the treaty is man's attempt to end the persecution or "trampling" of the Jews. The treaty will not end the persecution of God's people; it will only mark the beginning. Our Holy Scriptures are clear that the antichrist will carry out a holocaust against both Jews and Christians that will be worse than any slaughter the world has ever seen.

Isaiah 28:18-19:

> *"And your covenant with death shall be cancelled,*
> *And your pact with Sheol shall not stand;*
> *When the overwhelming scourge passes through,*
> *Then you become its trampling place.*
> *As often as it passes through, it will seize you.*
> *For morning after morning it will pass through,*
> *anytime during the day or night.*
> *And it will be sheer terror to understand what it means."*

Christ's Return as King

Assuming we have found the date the covenant will be signed, we can use this date to find the dates of other events that are prophesied. Please note we have speculated the antichrist will employ a false understanding of the riddle, so that he may declare himself the fulfilment of the prophecy to restore the holy place. The interpretation he will use is false; however, by understanding the false interpretation we can predict the date of an actual event, the making of the peace treaty prophesied in Daniel 9:27.

If indeed the peace treaty is made on Yom ha-Shoah, May 4th 1997, then other Scripture, if properly understood, will lead us to the date Christ will return as King. The date we will arrive at will agree with the correct understanding of the riddle, as well as the second and third timetables.

Most end time scholars agree the covenant to be made (Daniel 9:27) is a covenant of peace or a "peace treaty" made between Israel and her enemies. Some scholars understand the treaty to be one that is guaranteed by the antichrist; however, I believe the antichrist will instead be one of Israel's enemies and therefore a signor, rather than a guarantor, of the treaty.

Daniel 9:27 tells us that in the middle of the 7 year covenant the antichrist will *"put a stop to sacrifice and grain offering"*. He *"puts a stop"* to the re-established temple sacrifices when forces from him *"arise, desecrate the sanctuary fortress, and do away with the regular sacrifice"* (Daniel 11:31). If the treaty is signed on May 4th, 1997, then the exact middle day of the 7 year treaty will be November 2nd, 2000 (see Appendix (pages 87-93) for all calculations). The "doing away" or stopping of the temple sacrifices will therefore be on that day, November 2nd 2000.

In Daniel 12:6 a heavenly being asks the question, "How long will it be until the end of these wonders?" A close reading of this question and the two and a half chapters preceding it leads me to conclude the being is, in effect, asking when the return of Christ as King will be. Daniel may not have known that such was the core of this question, but nevertheless, believers today can deduce that is in fact the crux of the question. It is very clear, I believe, the "wonders" prophesied in Daniel 10-12 will not end until the Lord returns. The *"man dressed in linen"* answers the question twice - once with a riddle and once with a rather straightforward response. The first answer is that the end of the wonders will come after *"a time, times and half a time."* Understanding that riddle will provide the basis of Daniel's third timetable which I will explain in the last section of this paper. The second answer the man dressed in linen gives to Daniel's question is:

> **Daniel 12:11:** *"And from the time that the regular sacrifice is abolished, and the abomination of desolation is set up, there will be 1290 days."*

Since we have already calculated the date the sacrifice will be stopped or abolished, it is a simple matter to add 1,290 days and arrive at the date the *"wonders"* will end and Christ will return as King. That date is May 14th, 2004.

The Chart on page 37 depicts Daniel's first timetable.

Chart of Daniel's First Timetable

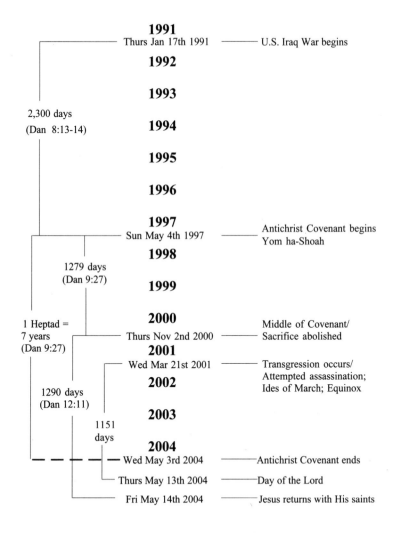

1991
Thurs Jan 17th 1991 ———— U.S. Iraq War begins

1992

1993

2,300 days
(Dan 8:13-14)　　**1994**

1995

1996

1997
Sun May 4th 1997 ———— Antichrist Covenant begins
1998　　　　　　　　　　Yom ha-Shoah

1279 days
(Dan 9:27)　　**1999**

1 Heptad =　　**2000**
7 years　　Thurs Nov 2nd 2000 ———— Middle of Covenant/
(Dan 9:27)　　　　　　　　　　Sacrifice abolished
2001
Wed Mar 21st 2001 ———— Transgression occurs/
Attempted assassination;
2002　　　　　　　　　　Ides of March; Equinox

1290 days
(Dan 12:11)　　**2003**

1151
days　　**2004**
Wed May 3rd 2004 ———— Antichrist Covenant ends
Thurs May 13th 2004 ———— Day of the Lord
Fri May 14th 2004 ———— Jesus returns with His saints

Daniel's Second Timetable
Daniel 9:25

The second timetable given to Daniel is the first of the three I understood and it is, I believe, the easiest one to understand. It is given to us in:

Daniel 9:25: *"So you are to know and discern that from the issuing of a decree to restore and rebuild Jerusalem until Messiah the Prince there will be seven weeks and sixty-two weeks; it will be built again, with plaza and moat, even in times of distress."*

This portion of the book of Daniel is written in Hebrew from the era of the Babylonian captivity, and because of the scarcity of Hebrew writings from that era, there is often uncertainty about the precise meaning of a number of words and phrases. Scholars often remark about how difficult it is to translate the Hebrew manuscripts from this period, and there is a great deal of scholarly debate about the exact meaning of much of the language they contain. In order to best understand the riddle Daniel 9:25 presents, it helps to look closely at several of the passage's words. It is not necessary to retranslate these words in order to solve the riddle. The N.A.S. version's translation is, in my opinion, excellent and certainly very accurate. However, if we put the following five words under a bit of a microscope, it will help to make the riddle even more clear:

Chathak - חתך *(#2852 Strong's numbering system):* Translated as *"decreed"* in Daniel 9:24, is a primitive root word that means to *"divide"* or *"cut out"*. Chathak is an uncommon word and this is its only use in the Old Testament.

Dabar - דבר *(#1697)* is a very common Hebrew word used hundreds of times in the Old Testament. In the N.A.S. version it is translated 833 times as *"word"* or *"words"*. It is translated as *"decree"* in only two places - here (Daniel 9:25) and 2 Chronicles 30:5. It is my opinion that the word *"decree"* is a little bit strong for the meaning here. Numerous scholars insist it is better to translate this phrase *"a word goes forth"* or *"a call goes forth"* or *"a proclamation is issued"*.

Shub - שוב *(#7725)* is another very common Hebrew word that is also used hundreds of times in the Old Testament. It means to turn back or return. The N.A.S. version translates it here as *"restore"*.

Shabua - שבוע *(#7620)* simply means *"seven"* or *"heptad"*. It was a word the Hebrews often used for "week", however, its basic meaning was more generic.

Charuts - חרוץ *(#2742).* Scholars are undecided about this seldom used word. Translators render it as **"moat", "wall", "trench", "ditch",** etc. Recently the word was found in the Dead Sea Scrolls and it has been translated there as **"conduit".** Evidently the word is one that conveys the meaning of carrying or transporting water, as with **"irrigation ditch".**

Daniel was given the prophecy contained in Daniel 9:24-27 in response to a marvellous prayer by Daniel that is recorded at the beginning of Chapter 9. In that prayer Daniel is deeply concerned about the future of his people and the Holy City, Jerusalem. Daniel had been reading the prophecies of Jeremiah (Jeremiah 25:11 and 29:10) which Daniel seems to have understood to be near fulfilment. Daniel and other Jews had been in captivity for approximately 68 years and Daniel expected Jeremiah's prophecy of 70 years of captivity to be fulfilled in the immediate future. It is clear Daniel is expecting an immediate restoration of the Holy City. Notice in verses 15-17 he asks the Lord to act *"now"*. He says, *"let now Thine anger and Thy wrath turn away from Thy city Jerusalem"* (verse 16) and *"so now ... O Lord, let Thy face shine on Thy desolate sanctuary".* 9 verse 17). Scholars have debated at great length whether or not Jeremiah's prophecy was precisely fulfilled. The Jews did, of course, return and Jerusalem was restored; however, attempts to calculate the exact period of captivity and compare it with Jeremiah's 70 years have been open to criticism. The main problem with each scholar's calculation is that the starting and ending points of the captivity are not clearly known, and thus it is difficult to prove precise fulfilment. Suffice it to say a number of scholars believe the specific prophecy in Jeremiah 25:11 and 29:10 has been fulfilled to the letter. It is very clear, however, that all Jeremiah's prophecies regarding Jerusalem's restoration have not yet been fulfilled. One good example is:

> **Jeremiah 24:7:** *"And I will give them a heart to know Me, for I am the Lord; and they will be My people, and I will be their God, for they will return to Me with their whole heart."*

That Jeremiah's prophecy concerning the specific "70 years" of captivity may have been fulfilled, however, does not mean Israel was fully restored and reconciled with God at the end of the 70 years of Babylonian captivity, which is the very clear message that Daniel is being given in 9:24-27. Gabriel is informing Daniel that although Jeremiah's 70 years are nearly completed, Daniel must understand that the complete restoration he is hoping for is many years yet future. Daniel surely understood this point after receiving this angelic visit, because he did not return with the captives. The message Daniel 9 is giving us is that the complete restoration of Israel will take many, many years. The underlying question Daniel is asking by his prayer is *"How long will it be until Jerusalem is fully restored?"* Daniel is given an answer to his question and that answer is: *"Israel will be fully restored when the Messiah comes".* Exactly when the Messiah will come is in the form of a riddle that can now, I believe, be correctly solved.

Many scholars have understood that Daniel 9:24 is informing Daniel that *"70 heptads"* are *"cut out"* of history during which time Israel will be waiting for her salvation and restoration. The Hebrew word, *"chathak"* is used in 9:24 and although the N.A.S. version translates it as *"decreed,"* a more precise understanding is the 70 heptads will be *"cut out".* The 70 sevens of years that Gabriel is referring to are *"cut out"* of an even longer historical time frame.

In verse 25, Daniel is given the riddle that answers the question implied by his prayer:

Daniel 9:25: (N.A.S.): *"So you are to know and discern that from the issuing of a* **call** *to* **return** *and rebuild Jerusalem until Messiah the Prince there will be seven* **heptads** *and sixty-two* **heptads***; it will be built again, with plaza and* **ditch,** *even in times of distress."*
(Note - emboldening of words is mine).

Most scholars who hold to the pretribulation rapture theory add the 7 heptads and 62 heptads together to come up with what is often called "Daniel's 69 weeks". They maintain that from the issuing of a decree by Artaxerxes given in 445B.C. (Nehemiah 2:5) until Christ entered Jerusalem to be crucified was exactly 483 (69 x 7) Biblical years. Sir Robert Anderson devised an interesting interpretation that attempts to calculate a fulfilment of this prophecy to the month. The claim that Anderson's work makes a calculation that is precise to the very day is inaccurate, since he assumes Nehemiah 2:1 is the first day of Nisan, while Nehemiah tells us only that it is *"the month Nisan"*. Some scholars use multiple exclamation marks when they refer to Anderson's work; however, a close examination of his calculations reveals major weaknesses and many scholars, including Walvoord, express reservations. Many scholars now believe he used a wrong date for Christ's crucifixion and that his theory has other timing errors.

Very few pretribulation rapture scholars seem to realize the 7 and 62 heptads should not be added together. One conservative scholar who understands why the Bible separates these heptads into two units is, of all people, Sir Isaac Newton. Approximately three hundred years ago, in a work that until only recently was long forgotten, Sir Newton explains the passage is prophesying two separate comings of the Lord. He tells us on page 137 of his reprinted book:

> *"Thus we have in this short prophecy, a prediction of all the main periods relating to the coming of the Messiah; the time of his birth, that of his death, that of the rejection of the Jews, the duration of the Jewish war whereby he caused the city and sanctuary to be destroyed, and the time of his second coming: and so the interpretation here given is more full and completed and adequate*

to the design, than if we should restrain it to his first coming only as interpreters usually do. We avoid also the doing violence to the language of Daniel by taking the seven weeks and sixty-two weeks for one number. Had that been Daniel's meaning, he would have said sixty and nine weeks and not seven weeks and sixty-two weeks, a way of numbering used by no nation."

That the passage is referring to two arrivals of the Lord is inferred also by the wording Gabriel used. Notice, for instance, Jerusalem will be rebuilt during *"times"* (plural) of distress. If this verse was predicting one return of the Jews and one rebuilding of Jerusalem, and therefore one coming of the Messiah, it would seem more natural to say it would happen during a *"time"* of distress rather than *"times"* of distress. In addition, the verse informs us Jerusalem will be built again with *"plaza and moat"* or *"plaza"* and *"ditch"*. Two examples of what will be rebuilt are given because each is representative of a separate restoration. The "plaza" or "square" represents the restoration that occurred in Nehemiah's day. The plaza was an important place in that day since the law was read there (Nehemiah 8:1). To Nehemiah and his contemporaries, the plaza symbolized the restoration of Jerusalem more than any other physical feature that was rebuilt. The *"ditch"* is referring, I believe, to the irrigation ditches Israel has built since 1948. These irrigation ditches have allowed the desert to bloom, and they represent the restoration that took place in 1948.

Daniel 9:25, therefore, is telling us there will be two "calls" issued for the Jews to return and rebuild Jerusalem, and two arrivals of the Messiah.

The sixty-two heptads prophesy the first coming of the Lord and the seven heptads prophesy when the Lord will come to rapture the saints. The immediate question, of course, is why doesn't the Bible say 62 heptads and 7 heptads rather than vice-versa? It would seem likely that if the 62 heptads is the time between a call and the first coming, then it should be the first number given, and the 7 heptads should be given to us second. The answer, I think, is because to the ancient Hebrews 62 and 7 might have been confused with 69 while 7 and 62 would not. When the smaller number followed the larger, it could mean the total was under consideration. The Hebrews did not have a word for 69 (just as we don't), and instead they would say "sixty and nine"; however, they would never say "nine and sixty". Gabriel did not want his message to indicate one unit of 69 heptads, so he reversed the order of the numbers. It is ironic modern scholars add them together anyway in order to accommodate a wrong interpretation. Note Gabriel's reversal of these two numbers does not alter the logic of the riddle. It is only our Western prejudices that tell us the riddle should follow a strict chronological order. The Hebrews often told a story or relayed an event where they would ignore the order of chronology that we from the West consider to be so important. The Bible has many other examples where chronological or sequential order seems reversed. For example:

> **Matthew 5:45:** *"in order that you may be sons of your Father who is in heaven; for He causes His sun to rise on the evil and the good, and sends rain on the righteous and the unrighteous."*

> **2 Corinthians 2:15-16:** *"For we are a fragrance of Christ to God among those who are being saved and among those who are perishing; to the one an aroma from death to death, to the other an aroma from life to life."*

The correct solution to this riddle is actually quite straight forward. If the correct "call" and the date it occurred is used, then exactly 434 years, or 62 heptads later to the day, is when Christ was born. The correct call, I am convinced, is not one made by a Gentile ruler. Scholars have looked intently at proclamations made by Artaxerxes, Cyrus, and Darius; but they have overlooked the call to return and rebuild Jerusalem made by Nehemiah in Nehemiah 11:1. The reason Nehemiah's call is ignored is threefold:

> **First:** Conservative scholars have, for the most part, accepted Sir Anderson's calculations. They have shown great enthusiasm for his solution, since they believe it works out so exactly, and they have not searched for an alternative.

> **Second:** History has not preserved the two important dates needed

to make the calculation; when Nehemiah made his call is open to question, and the birth date of Christ is also not agreed upon.

Third: The third reason is because the popular translations have translated "dabar" as "decree", which makes the passage sound like a formal proclamation is being issued by a ruler.

As already stated, history has not definitively preserved the date of Nehemiah's call, nor the birth date of Christ. If it had, no doubt, thousands would have easily solved the riddle, and it is apparent God does not want the solution to be either easy or obvious. If we look closely at the evidence available, however, I do believe we can know when Nehemiah made his call and when Jesus was born. Next we deal with an attempt to establish both dates.

Nehemiah's Call and Jesus' Birth

When did Nehemiah call for the return and rebuilding of Jerusalem? (Nehemiah 11:1)

Conservative scholars agree it was between 445B.C. and 433B.C., because Nehemiah was given permission to go to Jerusalem in the twentieth year of King Artaxerxes' reign (Nehemiah 2:1), and he remained there for 12 years (Nehemiah 5:14). There is debate about which year the call in 11:1 occurred; however, if we read the book in the natural way it is presented, the year appears to be near the end of his 12 year stay. The day given to us in Nehemiah 7:73 and 9:1, is 24 Tishri. If we assume the call was made on 24 Tishri, 436B.C. then Jesus should have been born exactly 434 years later, on 24 Tishri, 2 B.C.

When was Jesus Born?

Many scholars have maintained Jesus was born in 4 B,C., although there have been minority views that place His birth at various other dates. The 4 B.C. date that has been so accepted is largely based upon a comment by Josephus regarding the death of Herod, coupled with Luke's witness regarding Herod's slaughter of the newborns. The essence of the evidence is that Josephus mentions a lunar eclipse that occurred the year Herod died, and from Luke's account we know Herod was alive when Jesus was born. If Herod was alive when Jesus was born, and Herod died the year of the lunar eclipse, then Jesus had to have been born the year of the lunar eclipse or before. Scholars have believed the eclipse Josephus mentions was a partial one that occurred in 4 B.C., and therefore Jesus could not have been born after 4 B.C.

History records, however, a full lunar eclipse over Jerusalem that occurred on January 9th 1 B.C. In addition to the historical record, scientists have used computers to confirm the exact dates of ancient eclipses. Our modern computers are able to perform the complex and very extensive calculations necessary to predict not only the eclipses that will happen in the future, but also inform us of the ones we had in the past. The movements of our solar system are so precise that astronomers with modern computers can now know with great accuracy the exact positions of the heavenly bodies over enormous stretches of time. If the 1 B.C. lunar eclipse is the one Josephus referred to, then Herod would have died in 1 B.C. and Jesus could have been born as late as 1 B.C. without contradicting either Luke or Josephus.

The other main piece of evidence scholars have used to establish Christ's birth date is the census the Romans were taking when Jesus was born. Luke tells us Cyrenius was the governor of Syria when the census was taken, and scholars know Cyrenius held that position from 7 B.C. to 4 B.C. The logic that has been accepted for several hundred years is that if Jesus was born during the reign of Cyrenius, and Cyrenius' reign was from 7 B.C. to 4 B.C., then Jesus must have been born between 7 B.C. and 4 B.C. Recent archaeological evidence has now proven, however, Cyrenius was twice Governor of Syria and he also served from 4 B.C. to 1 B.C. Jesus, therefore, could have been born anytime between 1 B.C. and 7 B.C. without contradicting Luke.

The eclipse date and the reign of Cyrenius are the only two substantial bits of evidence scholars use to establish the 4 B.C. date; and since that evidence has been explained, many inquiring scholars are returning to the traditional date of 1-2 B.C. Some of the earliest Christian writers believed Jesus was born in the fall of 1 B.C. or 2 B.C. and the weight of modern scholarship is now considered by many to be in agreement with those early beliefs. Our modern calendar was developed by the Romans who had access to many records that have long since turned to dust and they believed Jesus was born in 1 B.C. In the 6th century a monk named Dionysius Exiguus computed Christ's birth to be the Roman year 754 (1 B.C.), and he had historical records available to him that no longer exist. We know that such records did exist then because Justin Martyr, a very respected early Christian writer, mentions the census records surrounding Christ's birth in Bethlehem. If those records did exist, then clearly Dionysius Exiguus had the hard evidence needed to establish Christ's birth date, and his conclusion that Jesus was born 1 B.C. should be given very strong consideration.

The year and day of our Lord's crucifixion is another date scholars have held various opinions on; however some scholars now hold it is an issue that has been definitively settled. If we know the date of Christ's crucifixion, then we can subtract his age, through a straight forward reading of Luke and John, and arrive at his birth date. An extremely convincing article written by Colin J. Humphreys and W.G. Waddington, Oxford University, concludes that Christ died on April 3rd, 33 A.D. They rely upon modern computers to help set the date, and they are convinced we know the date for certain. They make a number of very strong statements such as:

> *"If this evidence is accepted ...... A.D. 33 is the only possibility."*

> *"..... in our view the phrase 'the moon turned to blood' probably refers to the lunar eclipse, in which case the crucifixion can be dated unambiguously."*

> *"..... we have used calculations of occurrence of a lunar eclipse which, if accepted, allow the day, month and year of the crucifixion to be determined precisely."*

Many scholars conclude from the fourth Gospel that Christ's ministry was about 3½ years long. Luke tells us Jesus was *"about 30"* (Luke 3:23) when He was baptised at the beginning of His ministry. If Jesus was *"about 30"* when he started His ministry, then He would have been about 33½ when He died in April of 33 A.D. If He was about 33½ in April 33 A.D., then He would have been born in the fall of 2 B.C.

In addition to the above evidence, the Bible, I believe, gives us direct confirmation that Jesus was born between 1 and 2 B.C. via an understanding of the following riddle:

    a.   Abraham was born between 1948 and 1949 years after Adam, as can be known from a close examination of the book of Genesis. Henry Morris documents this Biblical truth in the index of his book **"The Genesis Record"**. (Henry Morris' purpose is not to shed light on the birth date of Jesus. He has an independent reason for his calculation).

b.   The birth of Abraham was the birth of Israel in the sense that Israel is a people and Abraham was its first person. In 1 Kings 8:16, for instance, God uses the phrase *"My people Israel"*. The Bible consistently considers the nation of Israel a particular group of people rather than a particular piece of land.

c.   Jesus is called the *"last Adam"* in 1 Corinthians 15:45.

d.   The modern nation of Israel was established in our calendar year 1948 (May 14th)

The Bible, therefore, seems to be providing us with a relationship, in riddle form, that can be expressed as follows:

The years between the birth of Adam and the birth of Abraham	=	The years between the birth of Jesus and the rebirth of Israel

OR

The years between the birth of the first Adam and the birth of the first Israel	=	The years between the birth of the last Adam and the birth of the last Israel

OR

1948½ years (approx)	=	1948½ years (approx)

The next question we need to consider is the day of the year Jesus was born. All indications seem to point to His birth being in the fall, and since Nehemiah's call was on 24th Tishri (our September/October), we should ask whether Jesus could have been born on exactly that date.

If the 24th Tishri was a Sabbath, although the exact calendar they used in that era can not be known for sure, but if it was a Sabbath, it would have been the Sabbath which in modern Jewish practice is called Sabbath Bereshit. Sabbath Bereshit marks the start of the new cycle of Torah readings and is symbolic of new beginnings. It would also directly follow the Feast of Tabernacles which is considered the "hinge to eternity" and symbolically stands at the end of time. The Feast of the Tabernacles looks toward the final redemption described by the prophet Zachariah. No other day of the year would better point to the birth of the Saviour than Sabbath Bereshit. It should also be noted Solomon's temple and the dedication of the alter was completed on the 23rd day of the 7th month (2 Chronicles 7:10). It seems appropriate Jesus would come to dwell with man on the same calendar month and day as the one which followed man's feeble attempt to build God a house.

If Nehemiah's call was in 436B.C. on 24th Tishri, and if Jesus was born on 24th Tishri, 2 B.C. then we have a simple solution to part of the riddle given to us in Daniel 9:25. The 62 heptads from the call until the Messiah prophesied the 434 years from Nehemiah's call to the first coming of the Lord. If our solution to this riddle is correct, then history will record another "call" to return and rebuild Israel, and 7 heptads after that call, or 49 years later, the Messiah will come again.

It should be noted there is also substantial reason to believe Jesus was born in the fall of 1B.C. If this is the case, then Nehemiah's call would have been made in 435B.C. Please note the exact dates for Nehemiah's call and Jesus' birth are still open to question and therefore it is not possible to be dogmatic regarding the solution of the first half of Daniel's Second Timetable. By contrast, the date needed to solve the second half of the Second Timetable is known for certain and thus its solution is firm.

Israeli Proclamation of Independence

This paper is claiming Jesus will come again exactly 7 heptads or 49 years after a modern day call to restore and rebuild Jerusalem. The second call which Daniel 9:25 prophesied was, I believe, made on May 14th 1948, in Israel's Proclamation of Independence. The following is a quote from that document:

> *"We call upon the Jewish people throughout the diaspora to join forces with us in immigration and construction, and to be at our right hand in the great endeavour to fulfil the age-old longing for the redemption of Israel."*

The above quote was found by my wife and me a number of months after I knew it must exist. I had already understood the first and second timetables, so I knew when the call should have been made and approximately what its message should be. We began our search looking through microfilm copies of old newspapers issued near the date Israel was re-established. I was expecting some sort of national announcement to have been reported by the press, but after a number of hours reading, we found nothing resembling a call to return to Jerusalem and rebuild the city. A word study I made months earlier had convinced me we were looking for a "call" or a "proclamation", rather than a decree and the message would be to "return and rubuild" rather than "restore and rebuild". After searching through the old papers we called up a number of books from the stacks we thought might hold the call for which we were looking. Mindy found a copy of the Israeli Proclamation of Independence in one of the books she was looking through, and when she brought it to my attention it took only a moment to realize she had found the call that Gabriel had prophesied 25 centuries earlier. The document actually used the word "call", which fit precisely with my word study, and it used the words "immigration and construction" for "return and rebuild". The call specifically asked the Jews to *"return and to be at our right hand in the great endeavour to fulfil the age-old longing for the redemption of*

Israel". The redemption and restoration of Israel is exactly what the 9th chapter of Daniel is all about. Note also the document ends with this confession *"With Trust in the Rock of Israel, we set our hands in witness to this proclamation"*. All Christians acknowledge the "Rock of Israel" is Jesus Christ. The Jews, for the most part, have not yet accepted Jesus as their Lord and Saviour, and they are not consciously referring to Him by this wording; yet, it is almost as if they realize He, ultimately, is their only hope.

Daniel 9:25 prophesies that 7 heptads, or 49 years after the call, Jesus will return as *"Messiah the Prince"*. 49 years after the date this call was issued will be May 14th 1997. The return of Jesus on May 14th 1997, however, will not be the Second Advent when our Lord returns to physically rule. Notice Daniel 9:25 calls him a *"Prince"*, not a King. This return will be what is normally called the "rapture". Note only 69 of Daniel's heptads will be completed at that point, and there will still be one more heptad to go before the Lord returns as King. The last 7 years, sometimes called "the great tribulation" (Matthew 24:21), starts immediately after the rapture takes place. It is also important to realize that the 7 year antichrist covenant mentioned in Daniel 9:27 is not the last or 70th week. Nearly all scholars add the 7 and 62 heptads of Daniel 9:25 to the one heptad of 9:27 and match them to the 70 heptads given in 9:24. This natural looking combination, however, is not a correct understanding of the riddle. The antichrist covenant is not made the day the rapture takes place, and it is not the first day of the great tribulation.

The great tribulation, or Daniel's 70th week, will begin immediately after the rapture. It seems, in fact, it will begin because of the rapture. Many conservative scholars believe the presence of the Holy Spirit currently acts as a restraint against evil and when He leaves earth, evil will be unrestrained. **2 Thessalonians 2:7** tells us:

> *"..... he who now restrains will do so until he is taken out of the way."*

The logic carries that when the saints depart, the indwelling Holy Spirit will leave with us, and when that takes place unrestrained evil and the start of the great tribulation will begin.

It is interesting to note that May 14th 1997, is exactly 1,335 days after Rosh Hashana ended in 1993. Many sincere Christians expected the rapture to happen during Rosh Hashana of that year, since that date seemed such a logical time for it to occur. Many early Christians, including Irenaeus, expected the millennium to begin in the year 2,000, and if the rapture were to take place in 1993, then there would have yet been 7 years left for the great tribulation. Rosh Hashana was considered a likely time of year for Christ's return, because it celebrates the Jewish New Year. Grant R. Jeffrey, in his book **"Armageddon, Appointment with Destiny"**, is careful to state he was not predicting when the rapture would take place; however, a close reading of his work left me with the inescapable conclusion he was expecting it to occur during Roah Hashana 1993 (September 16th & 17th). Jeffrey was not the only believer expecting the rapture to take place then, as a perusal of the various end time magazines and books will find that date to be one laden with expectation. A few years before I discovered Daniel's timetables, I was asked by a fellow Christian when I thought the rapture might take place. I answered by saying I did not know, but that my best guess was Rosh Hashana, 1993. It is a date that held great logic and symbolism and many Christians who study eschatology were expecting it to happen then. The rapture, of course, did not occur in 1993; however, it is interesting that Daniel 12:12 says "How blessed is he who keeps waiting and attains to the 1,335 days". The rapture will occur, I believe, exactly 1,335 days after Roah Hashana, 1993.

Summary of Daniel 9:24-27

The following is a brief summary of my understanding of Daniel 9:24-27, Daniel 12:12 and 2 Thessalonians 2:6-8:

1. There were two "calls" made to return and rebuild Jerusalem.

2. The first call was made by Nehemiah (Nehemiah 11:1) on 24th Tishri, 436B.C.

3. Jesus was born on 24th Tishri, 2 B.C., exactly 434 years (62 heptads) after the first call was issued.

4. The second call was made by the Jews who wrote the Israeli Proclamation of Independence, on May 14th 1948.

5. The return of Christ as Prince, when He comes to rapture the saints will be 49 years (7 heptads) after the second call. The rapture will take place on May 14th, 1997.

6. Daniel 12:12 may refer to the 1,335 days between Rosh Hashana, 1993, and the rapture on May 14th 1997.

7. The great tribulation starts immediately after the rapture.

8. Christ will return as King on May 14th 2004.

The chart on page 59 depicts what I believe to be the solution to the riddle given in Daniel 9:25.

Chart of Daniel's Second Timetable

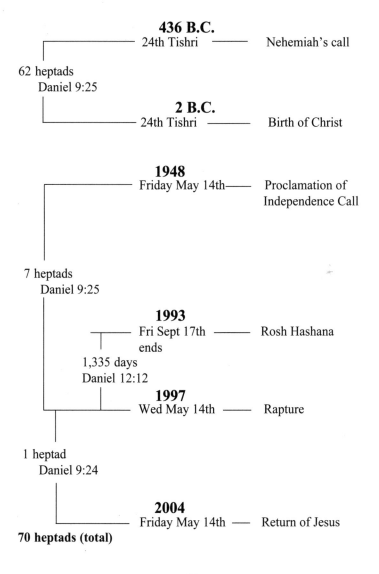

436 B.C.
24th Tishri ——— Nehemiah's call

62 heptads
Daniel 9:25

2 B.C.
24th Tishri ——— Birth of Christ

1948
Friday May 14th—— Proclamation of
Independence Call

7 heptads
Daniel 9:25

1993
Fri Sept 17th ——— Rosh Hashana
ends

1,335 days
Daniel 12:12

1997
Wed May 14th ——— Rapture

1 heptad
Daniel 9:24

2004
Friday May 14th —— Return of Jesus

70 heptads (total)

59

Daniel's Third Timetable Hidden by Design

An ever present theme in the book of Daniel is the question *"When will the holy place be restored?"* To the Jews of Daniel's day this question was understood in the narrow sense and was viewed to encompass the quest for the physical restoration of Jerusalem. God had unambiguously promised through the prophets before Daniel that He would restore Jerusalem. The jews were in captivity; they were slaves to the hated Babylonians, but they endured their misery by clinging to God's promise. They believed they would one day return to their land to again live under the blessings of the Lord of heaven and earth. Twenty-six centuries later we Christians are able to understand that the question which asks when the holy place will be restored is a much larger question than Daniel could possibly have imagined. We now have the New Testament and most end-time experts agree that Israel will never be restored in the fullest sense until Christ returns as King. The Jews quest for the restoration of their homeland is intrinsically tied into their acceptance of Jesus and His return to be King of all who believe in Him. Psalms 122:6 encourages us to *"pray for the peace of Jerusalem"*, and several strong members of our faith, including Kay Arthur and others, realize when we so pray, we are praying for the return of our Lord. There can be no peace and no final restoration until the Messiah returns to rule.

All three of Daniel's timetables are hidden by design. Daniel is told in Chapter 12, verse 9 that *"these words are concealed and sealed up until the end time"*. And, indeed, no truer words have ever been spoken. A multitude of scholars have attempted to unlock the secrets in Daniel, and one needs only to glance at their works to grasp the difficulties which they have encountered. Not only is the Hebrew often very obscure and difficult, but the book's logic and trains of thought never seem to go in an uninterrupted direction. The book is often used to teach simple messages to children, yet, at its deeper level it is a complicated maze of interlocking themes. The book asks questions which are answered in riddle form, and for over 2,500 years these riddles have withstood man's best attempts to understand them.

The first two timetables were unsolvable until certain modern events occurred. The nation of Israel had to be re-established before the second table could be found, and the U.S. war with Iraq provides an important date needed to understand the first table. The third timetable, by contrast, could actually have been solved in Daniel's day; however, it would have required insight that believers were not granted until the New Testament era. In a technical sense, the facts needed to solve the riddle were available to Daniel; however, he would have had to understand that before the Messiah will come to be King, there would be a first coming of the Lord and an "appearance" when Christ comes to rapture the saints. The Old Testament provides some hints that there would be a first and second coming, and I believe there are hidden references to the rapture; however, our modern understanding of these events comes from a study of the New Testament. It is possible, or even probable, however, that Christ was able to solve the third timetable. If such was the case, then he would have known what year and month He would return; however, He would not know the day because the particular day would yet depend upon calendar changes that had not yet occurred. Naturally, Christ could have known the day also, since He was God incarnate and therefore, capable of knowing all things; however, many times He limited Himself in the same kinds of ways that other humans are limited. I believe Jesus was able to understand the Old Testament as no other human could ever do, therefore, He was able to understand Daniel's third timetable. At the same time, He chose not to look into the future in order to know how the Jews would later change the Hebrew calendar; therefore He did not know the exact day He would return. He did not know the *"day or the hour"*. Note again Matthew 24:36 tells us that Jesus, while He was a man on earth, did not know the day or the hour He would return to set up His kingdom. I find it significant that it does not say He did not know the year or month. In addition, Jesus may have had knowledge about when the equinox occurs and therefore have been able to estimate a partial solution to the second timetable. The science of His day would not have been able to know the exact day on which a distant equinox would fall, so He would not have been able to use the second timetable to pinpoint the exact day of His return. It could have been used, however, to help confirm a solution to the third timetable. If Jesus had a perfect understanding of the Old Testament, He would have been able to solve the riddle that provides the third timetable, and He would have known the month and year of His return. I believe He did.

Daniel 12:6

The riddle that gives us Daniel's third timetable is the most difficult of the three to solve. Although the third timetable is independent of the other two, and therefore solvable by itself, I could not have solved it without first finding the first two tables. I had already found the date Jesus will return as King; therefore, I knew the riddle's answer before I understood how to solve it. Even though I knew the answer to the riddle, it still took me many months to solve the problems posed by that simple little sentence in Daniel. The question the riddle asks is:

Daniel 12:6: *"How long will it be until the end of these wonders?"*

The answer to this question is then given to us in the following verse

Daniel 12:7: *"..... for a time, times, and half a time;....."*

The question, in fact, being asked is *"When will Christ return as King?"* and the answer is *"after a time, times, and half a time"*.

In order to solve this riddle we need to solve four short problems

1. When does the riddle start, or as a scholar would say, when is the *"terminus a quo"*. In other words, what is the date at which the *"time, times, and half a time"* begin?

2. What length of time is being represented by the expression *"a time?"*

3. What length of time is being represented by the expression *"times?"*

4. What length of time is being represented by the expression *"half a time?"*

If the above four questions can be answered, then the riddle itself can be solved, and we will have the answer to when Jesus will return as King. The following is, I believe, the correct answer for each.

65

"Terminus a Quo"

The "terminus a quo" to this riddle is very straight forward. The time span the riddle gives us starts when the riddle is given. The man dressed in linen is saying in effect that the end of the wonders, and therefore the restoration of Israel and the arrival of the Messiah King, will be a "time, times and half a time" from the day he recites the riddle. We know from Daniel 10:1-4 this angelic and possibly theophanic visitation, which Daniel has relayed to us, came to him during the third year of Cyrus on the 24th day of the first month. Scholars debate a bit about when exactly this date is, but Joyce G. Baldwin understands it to be the 24th of Nisan, 537 B.C. I am confident her research and analysis are accurate.

The Hebrew Word "Moed"

The Hebrew word *"moed"* (Strongs #4150) is translated in Daniel 12:7 as a *"time"*. "Moed" is a rather specific term that does not have as broad a meaning as that which is carried by our English word "time". Moed usually means a "set" or "appointed" time such as the days that were set for the Hebrew feasts. It can mean a point in time or a duration of time. For our purpose here it most certainly represents some specific duration of time, and in order to solve the riddle we must determine to what duration of time the man dressed in linen is referring. It could refer to almost any duration, such as the years between the births of Adam and Jesus, the years between the destruction of the two temples, a solar year, etc, etc. The possibilities are endless, and there appears to be no clue as to which duration is the correct one.

Many conservative scholars have maintained a 360 day "prophetic year" is the duration to which the riddle is referring. They interpret the *"time"* to be equal to 360 days, the *"times"* to be 720 days, and the *"half a time"* to equal 180 days. Added together the total is 1,260 days or 3½ "prophetic" years. They arrive at this interpretation by comparing the riddle with Revelation 12:14, which uses a very similar phrase (although the Daniel phrase is in Hebrew and Revelation is in Greek) and concluding the two phrases are referring to the 1,260 days mentioned in Revelation 12:6. These scholars then usually believe the "time, times, and half a time" is a 1260 day time-frame that refers to the last half of the 7 year tribulation period. One of the problems with understanding the riddle in this way, however, is the answer just does not fit the question being asked. The question is: *"How long will it be until the end of these wonders?"* It is a nonsequitur to answer that question by saying *"The last half of the 7 year tribulation will be 1,260 days"*. The scholars that hold this interpretation attempt to overcome this objection by maintaining the "wonders" refer to end time details prophesied in the previous chapter and linking those prophesies to the *"time of distress"* mentioned in Daniel 12:1; but they do not, in my opinion, adequately establish their position.

The *"time"* of Daniel 12:7 refers, I believe, to the time that elapsed between Genesis 1:2 and Genesis 8:11. Genesis 1:2 describes the first moment of creation when the Holy Spirit moved over the surface of the waters, and **Genesis 8:11** depicts the moment when the dove Noah released returned to him with a freshly picked olive leaf in her beak.

The 8th chapter of Genesis provides us with a chronology of the events surrounding Noah's time spent in the ark, and chronicles the point at which he sent the dove out for the second time to search for dry land. The N.A.S. version translates this verse as follows:

> **Genesis 8:11:** *"And the dove came to him toward evening and behold in her beak was a freshly picked olive leaf. So Noah knew that the water was abated from the earth."*

The Interlinear's literal version reads as follows:

> *"And came in to him the dove the time of the evening. And, behold, an olive leaf newly plucked in her mouth! So knew Noah that had receded the waters from off the earth."*

When my research led me to this verse I realized almost immediately the time span I was searching for was the time between the doves moving over the water! The dove symbolically represents the Holy Spirit (Matthew 3:16), and Genesis 1:2 provides for us the first time the Holy Spirit moved over the water:

> **Genesis 1:2:** *"And the earth was formless and void, and darkness was over the surface of the deep; and the Spirit of God was moving over the surface of the waters."*

The riddle given to us in Daniel 12:6-7 uses this span of time, from the first day of creation until the dove returns with the olive branch, as the span expressed by "moed". It is easy to appreciate the Lord's choice of this span of time, since the symbolism is readily apparent. The dove bringing back the olive branch was the sign God provided Noah to assure him that a new creation had started. God had destroyed His old creation by the flood, and the dove returning with her branch marked the beginning of a new creation, and the ending of the era that God had put to an end by the flood. The dove arriving with the olive branch is the point that marks the moment when from Noah's point of view, the antediluvian world changes into the postdiluvian world. The time span between the two doves flying over the waters is the time span that the "old world" or the antediluvian world endured and it is that span of time used by the riddle as a part of the span of time that will pass before the millennium begins.

In order to solve the riddle therefore, it is necessary to find how much time elapsed between the "flights of the two doves". How many years, months, and days did the antediluvian world endure?

When I turned to my commentaries and other scholarly sources to find the length of the time span between Genesis 1:2 and 8:11, I quickly found there is no expert consensus. Various experts express various opinions on the matter, but the problem is they almost never agree. The difficulty lies with unscrambling the chronology provided in Genesis 7 and 8 and with understanding the Patriarchal calendar provided by Genesis 5. The Patriarchal calendar is a calendar quite different than any modern system man uses to keep track of time. Since the experts didn't agree, I set out on a study to make my own calculations. The following is my personal calculation of the time span that elapsed between Genesis 1:2 and Genesis 8:11. This analysis runs through to page 77.

Genesis 5 provides us an ancient calendar that chronicles the lives of the patriarchs from the creation of Adam through the birth of Noah's 3 sons. Many scholars assume Genesis 5 does not intend to supply for us a time line that is accurate to the year. They maintain Genesis 5 is not meant to be a precise calendar and that it can only be used to make estimates of chronological points in time. They arrive at this conclusion because Genesis 5 cannot provide us with a precise time line, *unless it uses a different method than any modern system*. It is my contention that Genesis 5 is a very precise calendar and we need to make only three assumptions, all of which are Scripturally based, in order to recreate a calendar that accurately reflects the ancient world up through the great flood. These three assumptions are as follows:

1.   The Patriarchal Calendar begins with the creation of Adam

rather than the first day of creation, which was five days earlier. Genesis 5 is clearly based on the births and lives of the patriarchs, and it is only logical and consistent the first day of this calendar coincides with the first day of man on earth. Genesis 5:1 states *"This is the book of the generations of Adam. In the day when God created man. He made him in the likeness of God".* The phrase *"In the day when God created man"* informs us, I believe, that the "book of generations" begins on the day Adam was created. In addition, Jewish tradition holds that their ancient calendar begins at the creation of Adam rather than the creation of the world. Our modern calendar begins with the birth of Jesus, who in 1 Corinthians 15:45 is called the *"last Adam".* The calendar it replaced began with the first Adam. The first day of the calendar was the day God created Adam, and the first day of each subsequent year was therefore the same as Adam's birthday.

2.   The most ancient calendars used a 360 day year. This is evident from a number of Bible passages as well as secular sources, and scholars are in agreement they contained 12 months of 30 days each. Most secular scholars maintain man just did not make accurate enough measurements and simply missed the count by approximately 5¼ days. Such a position is not very tenable, however, since it does not take modern instruments to measure the year closer than to within 5¼ days. I believe the ancient year actually contained only 360 days and the length of our year was altered by the great flood. Evidently the earth's rotation and course around the sun were altered by the shifting water, and we ended up with a curiously tilted axis and a year that is slightly under 365¼ days long.

3.   The passage assumes we realize the "years" referred to are calendar years which were based upon Adam's birthdate, not years based on the birth dates of each individual patriarch. When modern man says a particular person became a father at, say, age 31, what we mean is starting from that individual's birth date, he lived 31 full solar years and then became a father sometime during his 32nd year. It is certain the ancients did not use the same method as we do, because if they did then Genesis 7:6 does not agree with

72

Genesis 7:11. There is a subtle but very important point that can be understood if one carefully reads these two verses. Notice Genesis 7:6 says the flood came when Noah was 600 years old. In English, using our system of keeping track of a person's years, this statement means Noah had lived 600 full solar years and the flood occurred sometime during the 601st solar year of his life. Verse 11, however, tells us it was "in" or during his 600th year. To harmonise these two verses, we have to realize the ancients were not using the same system we use to keep track of their life spans. Instead of using their own birthdays, the ancients used a calendar year based upon Adam's birthday as their basis to start the count. They would start an individual's life span count at the start of the first full calendar year after the individual's birth, and then would include the calendar year during which his child was born. As a result of this method of keeping track of time, when the Bible says in Genesis 5:6, for instance, *"Seth lived one hundred and five years, and became the father of Enosh"*, it means Enosh was born during the 105th full calendar year after the birth of Seth. If they were using our method, then the entire chapter is hopelessly ambiguous, and we cannot use it for anything more than a rough count. It seems safe to assume the ancients were smart enough to be using a system that would keep an accurate record, since the primary purpose of the chapter is to provide us with a record of the life spans of the patriarchs. If they left us with a record that provides us with accurate and precise information, then they had to be using the method I have described above. **No other method**, at least none I have been able to imagine, will work. I am confident the passage must be assuming the full calendar year system I have described, because the only alternative is that the passage is incomplete and ambiguous. I believe all Scripture is inspired and designed for our use, and therefore Genesis 5 provides us with an accurate and precise table of dates from which we can construct an ancient calendar. The ancient calendar we can construct using Genesis 5 will be given after we unscramble the chronology of the events surrounding the flood given to us in Genesis 7 and 8.

Genesis 7 and 8 provide for us a chronology of certain events that occurred during the Great Flood. The passage is difficult to sort out and scholars do not agree on how to understand it. The passage is difficult because, as explained earlier, the dating system was different then, but also notice the water seems to dry up three different times. The water is *"dried up"* by Genesis 8:7 and yet Noah sends a dove out in verse 8 *"to see if the water was abated from the face of the land"*. The water, although dried up in verse 7, is still *"on the surface of all the earth"* in verse 9. In verse 11 it has abated, and by verse 13 it is again said to be dry; then in verse 14, which is the 57th day following the *"dried up"* ground of verse 13, we are told *"the earth was dry"*. The Bible is obviously categorizing different degrees of dryness. One degree is dry enough for the raven, another for the dove, and a third for Noah and his family. If we correctly sort out the details of these chapters, we can calculate the exact day the dove was sent out the second time (verse 11) and therefore find the exact length of time that is meant by *"a time"* (moed) as it is used in the riddle given in Daniel 12:6-7. The following is a table I believe represents the information we are given by this passage:

Event	Flood Day	Calendar			Scripture
		Mth	Day	Year	
God spoke		2	10	1656	6:13-7:4
Flood begins	1	2	17		7:11
Last day of rain	40	3	26		7:12
Water prevailed	150	7	16		7:24
Ark rested	151	7	17		8:4
Mt tops visible	225	10	1		8:5
Sends raven	264	11	10		8:6-7
Water dries	315	1	1	1657	8:13
Dove sent 1st time	322	1	8		8:8
Dove sent 2nd time	329	1	15		8:10-11
Dove sent 3rd time	336	1	22		8:12
God spoke	371	2	27		8:14-17

The following is a line-by-line explanation of how the above table was derived:

God Spoke: We know from Genesis 7:4 God spoke to Noah on the 8th day before the rains were sent. Since He sent the rains on 2/17 (verse 11), we know He spoke on 2/10.

Flood Begins: Genesis 7:11 tells us the flood began on 2/17 in the 600th year of Noah's life. In English this reads as if Noah was in his 600th solar year of life when the flood began on 2/17 of that year. This verse cannot mean as such, however, since it would then contradict verse 6. In the ancient system "Noah's 600th year" referred to a particular calendar year, not the solar years of Noah's individual life span. The year is 1656 as can be calculated from the information given by chapter 5. (See Appendix for all calculations.)

Last Day of Rain: The rain fell for 40 days and 40 nights (Genesis 7:12). The months were all 30 days long, so the last day of rain was on 3/26.

Water Prevailed: The water prevailed for 150 days, or 5 months (Genesis 7:24), so it stopped prevailing on 7/16. 7/16 is 150 days after the flood began.

Ark Rested: At the end of the 150 days that the water prevailed, the water began to decrease (Genesis 8:3). The water decreased because the ocean basins began to give way and the water ran off to collect in the depths thereby created. At day 151, on 7/17, the Ark rested on the mountains of Ararat. (Genesis 8:4).

Mountain Tops Visible: The water decreased steadily; on 10/1 the mountain tops surrounding the Ark were visible. (Genesis 8:5).

Sends Raven: At the end of 40 days Noah opened a window and sent out a raven on 11/10 (Genesis 8:6-7). Noah kept sending the raven which flew "here and there" or "back and forth" until the water dried up. (Genesis 8:7).

75

The Water Dried Up: The water dried up "in the six hundred and first year, in the first month, on the first of the month" (Genesis 8:13). The 601st year is, of course, a reference to Noah's life span. It is the 601st full **calendar year** of his life. It is not his 601st solar year. We keep time in that manner, but the ancients based their life spans on the calendar. The first day of the first month, therefore, is not a reference to Noah's birthday, but rather refers to "New Years Day" of the year 1657. The water dried up, therefore, on 1/1/1657. The water was "dried up" enough by 1/1/1657 that the raven, evidently, failed to return. Scholars believe Noah sent a raven first because a raven is less particular than a dove and would land on ground that was muddy. When the raven failed to return, Noah then reasoned it was time to send out a dove.

Dove Sent First Time: Noah did not send out the dove for the first time until 7 days after the raven failed to return. Scholars are in agreement the 7 day waiting period is implied by verse 10 where it says he waited *"another seven days"* before he sent the dove out the second time. The Hebrew uses terminology translated here as *"another seven days"* and scholars agree it refers back to an unspoken, yet implied, seven days he waited before he sent the dove out the first time. Noah therefore sent the dove out for the first time on 1/8/1657. (Genesis 8:8).

Dove Sent Second Time: This is the very important date we have spent so must effort to find. Genesis 8:10-11 tells us Noah waited *"another seven days"* and then sent the dove out again. The dove was sent out, therefore, on 1/15/1657. She returned to Noah with a freshly plucked olive leaf in her beak *"toward evening"* on that date.

Dove Sent Third Time: Genesis 8:12 tells us Noah waited yet another seven days before sending the dove out for a third time on 1/22/1657. This time she did not return.

God Spoke: The chronology ends just as it began, with God speaking. On 2/27/1657 God spoke again to Noah and told him the earth was dry enough for Noah and his family to depart. (Genesis 8:14-17).

Finally! The dove was sent out for the second time on 1/15/1657! Remember Adam was created on 1/1/1, and therefore, the Holy Spirit moved over the waters (Genesis 1:2) five days earlier. The "time between the doves", therefore, must include these extra 5 days. Note, 1/15/1657 is 15 days into the 1657th year; therefore, 1656 full calendar years have elapsed. The "time between the doves", the *"moed"* of Daniel 12:7, is therefore 1656 years, plus 15 days, plus 5 days, or 1656 years, 20 days. The antideluvian world can be understood to begin on the first day of creation and end when the dove brought back the olive leaf. The olive leaf, of course, represents God's promise of a new postdiluvian world. The antediluvian world, therefore, lasted for 1656 years and 20 days, and it is the time span or *"moed"* incorporated in the riddle which gives us Daniel's third timetable. See the Appendix for the Ancient Calendar constructed by this analysis.

We have now concluded what is meant by the expression *"a time"* in the answer to the riddle given in Daniel 12:6-7. The question asked is *"How long will it be until the end of these wonders?"* The word translated by the N.A.S. as *"wonders"* is the Hebrew word *"pele"* (Strongs #6382) and it means *"extraordinary, hard to be understood"* and is often used in association with God's acts of judgment and redemption (see page 810 of **"The New Brown-Driver-Briggs-Gesenius Hebrew-English Lexicon"**). The answer to that question, as stated earlier in this paper, is *"when Jesus returns as King"* and that, we are told, will be in *"a time, times, and half a time"*. We have now answered the first and second questions posed on page 65. We have decided when the riddle begins and what the riddle means by *"a time"*. Now, in order to complete solving the riddle, we must decide what is meant by *"times,* and *"half a time"*, the third and fourth questions posed on page 65.

77

The Hebrew Word "Moedim"

The word translated here as "times" is the Hebrew word moedim, which is the plural of moed. The "times" of the riddle is the plural of the "time", however, it represents a different time span. As stated previously, it is a word that means "appointed times". It is often used in connection with the appointed feasts and it means a time span "set" or "predetermined". The word is used, for instance

> **Habakkuk 2:3:** *"For the vision is yet for the appointed time;*
> *It hastens toward the goal, and it will not fail.*
> *Though it tarries, wait for it;*
> *For it will certainly come, it will not delay."*

Very early in my quest to solve this riddle, I understood the *"times"* of Daniel 12:7 referred to the 8 heptads or 56 years that remain after the passing of the 62 heptads given in Daniel 9:25. In other words, the "appointed times" began when the nation of Israel was reborn on May 14th 1948. Remember back to when we solved the riddle which provided for us Daniel's second timetable. That riddle is given to us in Daniel 9:25 and it prophesies that after the 62 heptads the Messiah will come, and then at a later time the Jews will again return and rebuild Jerusalem. The second return, as all the world witnessed in 1948, marks the beginning of the 8 heptads that had been "cut out" and reserved for the last days. Those 8 heptads, or 56 years, are the appointed times, represented by the word "moedim". Just as the "moed" of this riddle represents an extremely important time span from our world's history, so also does the "moedim". The end-time return of the Jews to their land is considered by nearly all pretribulation scholars to be the most important fulfilment of prophecy since the birth of our Lord. Many, many passages of Scripture make it abundantly clear the Jews would be back in their land, thus fulfilling their role in end-time events. It should be considered a modern miracle that a race of people who had no nation for centuries, and who were persecuted for most of that time somehow survived as a distinct people that would stream back to a homeland they had been driven from so long before. They were driven to every corner of the earth, persecuted, slaughtered, and despised; and just exactly as Isaiah, Jeremiah and Zechariah, and the other prophets told us - they went back. The world witnessed them go back in our generation and I am convinced we are the generation that *"will not pass"* (Matthew 24:34) until Christ returns to rule.

When the disciples of Jesus asked Him, *"What will be the sign of Your coming?"* (Matthew 24:3) He alerted them, and us, to many perils that would come upon the world. He did answer their question, though, when He told them to *"learn the parable from the fig tree"* (Matthew 24:32). Numerous scholars have understood the fig tree represents Israel and that her rebirth in 1948 was a fulfilment of the prophecy that says *"When its branch has already become tender, and puts forth its leaves"* (Matthew 24:32). The disciples were told when they saw that occur, along with the other prophecies of Matthew 24, they were to recognize *"He is near, right at the door"*.

The *"appointed times"*, therefore, are the 8 heptads, or 56 years prophesied in Daniel 9:24-25 and which began on May 14th, 1948.

We have now concluded *"a time"* is equal to 1656 years, and 20 days, and that *"times"* is equal to 56 years. We have only to decide what *"half a time"* is and we can add them all together to provide the solution to the riddle. "Half a time" is the easiest part of the riddle, since scholars agree it refers back to the *"time"* or *"moed"* rather than to the *"times"* or *"moedim"*. It is, in other words, *"half a time"*, just as it is translated and not "half a times". Half a time is half of 1656 years and 20 days, or 828 years and 10 days.

The solution to the riddle is as follows:

"a time"	=	1,656 years, 20 days
"times"	=	56 years
"half a time"	=	828 years, 10 days
TOTAL:		2,540 years, 30 days

The question asked was *"How long will it be until the end of these wonders?"* That question was asked on 24th Nisan, 537 B.C. (Daniel 10:1-4) and it is asking in effect,

"When will Jesus return as King?"

The answer is:

"He will return after 'a time, times and half a time'."

He will return 2,540 years and 30 days after 24th Nisan, 537 B.C. That day, as per the modern Hebrew Calendar, will be 23 Iyyar, 5764.

23 Iyyar 5764 is May 14th, 2004.

See the following Chart which depicts Daniel's Third Timetable.

Chart of Daniel's Third Timetable

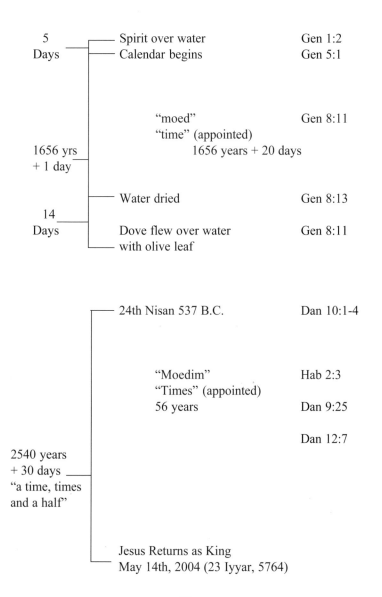

5
Days
— Spirit over water   Gen 1:2
— Calendar begins   Gen 5:1

"moed"   Gen 8:11
"time" (appointed)
1656 years + 20 days

1656 yrs
+ 1 day

— Water dried   Gen 8:13

14
Days

Dove flew over water   Gen 8:11
— with olive leaf

24th Nisan 537 B.C.   Dan 10:1-4

"Moedim"   Hab 2:3
"Times" (appointed)
56 years   Dan 9:25

Dan 12:7

2540 years
+ 30 days
"a time, times
and a half"

Jesus Returns as King
May 14th, 2004 (23 Iyyar, 5764)

Conclusion

Each of Daniel's timetables provide us with the exact same day, May 14th, 2004, when Jesus will return as King. In addition, they find for us the day the rapture will occur, the day the antichrist will sign a 7 year covenant, and the day an attempt on the antichrist's life will be made. The tables are confirmed by the fact they agree with one another, and they are in harmony with a birth date for Jesus that seems most likely. The treaty date happens to fall on Yom ha-Shoah, the "Day of Holocaust", a day which seems so fitting, and the assassination attempt is made during the night of the Spring Equinox on the first day of the Ides of March.

When Rosh Hashana 1993 ended, there were exactly 1,335 days left before the rapture, just as Daniel 12:12 informs us, and the "call" that went forth for the return to, and rebuilding of, Jerusalem was fulfilled precisely by the language of "Israel's Proclamation of Independence". The "moed" of the Daniel 12:6 riddle is the time span the antediluvian world endured. The "moedim" (appointed times) began with the blossoming of the fig tree.

The book of Daniel has been my constant companion for many years. I believed very early it contained secrets that would be held until the end times and that these secrets would soon be known by the faithful. There were many times when my search seemed futile and I would lay my work down for weeks and months at a time. I always picked it back up, however, and I was continually driven in my search to understand by the encouragement that one day *"those who have insight will understand"*. (Daniel 12:10)

The Lord has told us He will return for us and I believe the day is drawing near.

Appendix

The Riddle of the
2,300 Evenings and Mornings

In order to solve the riddle given at Daniel 8:13-14, we must first answer 4 questions

1. What question is the riddle asking?
2. When do the 2,300 evenings and morning begin?
3. How long a time is 2,300 evenings and mornings?
4. What does the Hebrew word "tsadeq" mean? (Strongs #6663)

The above 4 questions, if answered correctly, will solve the riddle. The question, however, can be answered incorrectly, which will result in an incorrect solution to the riddle. Correctly understood, this riddle will point to Jesus Christ as Messiah. If it is incorrectly understood, it will point to the coming antichrist.

Question	Correct Answer	Incorrect Answer
What question is the riddle asking?	How long will it be from the committing of the transgression (verse 12) until the vindication of the holy place? (verse 14)	How long will it be from the start of the conflict between the ram and the goat (vs6) and vindication (a false one) of the holy place. (verse 14)
When do the 2300 evenings & mornings begin?	When the transgression is committed. (verse 12)	When the conflict between the ram and the goat begins. (verse 6)
How long a time is 2300 evenings and mornings?	1150 evenings + 1150 mornings, spanning 1151 days.	2300 days.
What does the Hebrew word "tsadeq" mean?	Vindication of Israel (Jerusalem) on the Day of the Lord.	Vindication (a false one) of Israel (Jerusalem) when covenant made.

A False Vindication

The following calculates the "false vindication" of the holy place. The antichrist will interpret Daniel 8:13-14 to be a prophecy which predicts 2300 days will elapse between the start of the war between the ram and the goat (Daniel 8:1-7) and the antichrist's "peace treaty". The antichrist will declare that his treaty is the prophesied vindication of the holy place. When he claims to be the vindicator of Israel, the antichrist is in effect claiming to be God, since numerous Bible passages make it clear that Israel's vindication will come from the Lord.

January 17th 1991 thru January 16th 1992	=	365 days
January 17th 1992 thru January 16th 1993	=	366 days(leap year)
January 17th 1993 thru January 16th 1994	=	365 days
January 17th 1994 thru January 16th 1995	=	365 days
January 17th 1995 thru January 16th 1996	=	365 days
January 17th 1996 thru January 16th 1997	=	366 days(leap year)
January 17th 1997 thru May 4th 1997	=	108 days

(Jan 15; Feb 28; Mar 31; Apr 30; May 4)

Total:	**2300 days**

Therefore, 2300 days from January 17th 1991 is May 4th 1997

Conclusion:

According to a false interpretation, the holy place (Israel) will be "vindicated" on **May 4th 1997,** when the antichrist makes the peace treaty.

This day is also the day in 1997 when Israel will celebrate "Yom ha-sho'ah" (Day of Holocaust).

Peace Treaty Middle

Although the peace treaty will not be Israel's true vindication, it will still be an historical date which the Bible prophesies. The following calculates the exact middle day of that 7 year treaty.

The "vindication" of Israel (Daniel 8:14), according to the antichrist, will be when he makes a covenant or peace treaty with her (Daniel 9:27)

The treaty will be 7 years long (Daniel 9:27).

In the middle of the treaty, the antichrist will abolish the Regular Sacrifice (Daniel 9:27 and 11:31).

May 4th 1997 thru May 3rd 1998	=	365 days
May 4th 1998 thru May 3rd 1999	=	365 days
May 4th 1999 thru May 3rd 2000	=	366 days (leap year)
May 4th 2000 thru May 3rd 2001	=	365 days
May 4th 2001 thru May 3rd 2002	=	365 days
May 4th 2002 thru May 3rd 2003	=	365 days
May 4th 2003 thru May 3rd 2004	=	366 days (leap year)
Total:		**2557 days in 7 years**

Therefore:
> **1278 days +1 (middle days) + 1278 days = 2557 days in 7 years**

> So the middle of the 7 year peace treaty is day number 1279, from May 4th 1997, calculated as follows:

May 4th 1997 thru May 3rd 1998	=	365 days
May 4th 1998 thru May 3rd 1999	=	365 days
May 4th 1999 thru May 3rd 2000	=	366 days (leap year)
May 4th 2000thru Nov 2nd 2000	=	183 days
(May 28; Jun 30; Jul 31; Aug 31;		
Sep 30; Oct 31; Nov 2; = 183)		
Total:		**1279 days**

Conclusion:
> The middle day of the peace treaty, when the sacrifice will be abolished, is **November 2nd 2000.**

The End of the Age

Once we know when the middle of the treaty is, then we can calculate when the end of the age will be. The sacrifice is stopped at the mid point of the treaty (Daniel (9:27) and the end of the age is 1290 days after the sacrifice is stopped (Daniel 12:11).

Go to Daniel 12:11. From the abolishing of the sacrifice (November 2nd 2000, to the end of the age (note verse 6) there will be 1290 days.

Nov 2nd 2000 thru Dec 31st 2000	=	60 days
(Nov 29; Dec 31; = 60 days)		
Jan 1st 2001 thru Dec 31st 2001	=	365 days
Jan 1st 2002 thru Dec 31st 2002	=	365 days
Jan 1st 2003 thru Dec 31st 2003	=	365 days
Jan 1st 2004 thru May 14th 2004	=	135 days
(Jan 31; Feb 29; Mar 31;		
Apr 30; May 14; = 135)		
Total:		**1290 days**

Conclusion:

The end of the age is **May 14th 2004.** Jesus will return to earth with His saints (1 Thessalonians 3:13) on that day. That day also happens to be the 56th anniversary of the re-establishment of the state of Israel. The last 8 heptads, *"The appointed times"* are over and the millennium begins.

Date of the Transgression

Now, let us go back to Daniel 8:13-14 and correctly interpret the riddle.

2300 evenings and morning is like saying 2300 dinners and breakfasts which would be 1150 dinners and 1150 breakfasts, and would therefore span 1151 of our modern days (since we start the day in the middle of the night).

The Day of the Lord is May 13th 2004
Back off 1151 days from May 13th 2004:

May 13th 2004 thru Jan 1st 2004	=	134 days
(May 13; Apr 30; Mar 31; Feb 29; Jan 31)		
Dec 31st 2003 thru Jan 1st 2003	=	365 days
Dec 31st 2002 thru Jan 1st 2002	=	365 days
Dec 31st 2001 thru Mar 20th 2001	=	287 days
(Dec 31; Nov 30; Oct 31; Sep 30; Aug 31;		
Jul 31; Jun 30; May 31; Apr 30; Mar 12)		
Total:		**1151 days**

Conclusion:

Israel will be vindicated at the day of the Lord; and the transgression that causes horror will occur 1151 days before on the night of **March 20th 2001.**

Note that the night of March 20th 2001 includes the first 6 hours of March 21st 2001.

The Year of the Flood

Genesis 5 and 7 give us enough information to calculate the year that Noah's Flood began. The following calculation demonstrates that the rains fell during the 1,656th year after the creation of Adam:

130   Age of Adam when Seth was born (Gen 5:3)

105   Age of Seth when Enosh was born (Gen 5:6)

90   Age of Enosh when Kenan was born (Gen 5:9)

70   Age of Kenan when Mahalaleel was born (Gen 5:12)

65   Age of Mahalaleel when Jared was born (Gen 5:15)

162   Age of Jared when Enoch was born (Gen 5:18)

65   Age of Enoch when Methuselah was born (Gen 5:21)

187   Age of Methuselah when Lamech was born (Gen 5:25)

182   Age of Lamech when Noah was born (Gen 5:28)

600   Age of Noah when Flood began (Gen 7:6)

When these ancient records refer to the age of a Patriarch at his son's birth, they are not using the same method of age calculation that we use. Instead of using individual birth dates, the ancients used Adam's creation date as the basis from which to begin the age counts that Genesis 5 and 6 record. A fuller explanation of their system is explained in the body of this paper.

Ancient Calendar

Month	1	2	3	4	5	6	7	8	9	0	11	12	1	2	3
							1656							**1657**	
Sun							1							1	
Mon	-	-	-	1	-	-	2	-	-	-	1	-	-	2	-
Tue	1	-	-	2	-	-	3	1	-	-	2	-	-	3	1
Wed	2	-	-	3	1	-	4	2	-	-	3	1	-	4	4
Thu	3	1	-	4	2	-	5	3	1	-	4	2	-	5	3
Fri	4	2	-	5	3	1	6	4	2	-	5	3	1	6	4
Sat	5	3	1	6	4	2	7	5	3	1	6	4	2	7	5
Sun	6	4	2	7	5	3	8	6	4	2	7	5	3	8	6
Mon	7	5	3	8	6	4	9	7	5	3	8	6	4	9	7
Tue	8	6	4	9	7	5	10	8	6	4	9	7	5	10	8
Wed	9	7	5	10	8	6	11	9	7	5	10	8	6	11	9
Thu	10	8	6	11	9	7	12	10	8	6	11	9	7	12	10
Fri	11	9	7	12	10	8	13	11	9	7	12	10	8	13	11
Sat	12	10	8	13	11	9	14	12	10	8	13	11	9	14	12
Sun	13	11	9	14	12	10	15	13	11	9	14	12	10	15	13
Mon	14	12	10	15	13	11	16	14	12	10	15	13	11	16	14
Tue	15	13	11	16	14	12	17	15	13	11	16	14	12	17	15
Wed	16	14	12	17	15	13	18	16	14	12	17	15	13	18	16
Thu	17	15	13	18	16	14	19	17	15	13	18	16	14	19	17
Fri	18	16	14	19	17	15	20	18	16	14	19	17	15	20	18
Sat	19	17	15	20	18	16	21	19	17	15	20	18	16	21	19
Sun	20	18	16	21	19	17	22	20	18	16	21	19	17	22	20
Mon	21	19	17	22	20	18	23	21	19	17	22	20	18	23	21
Tue	22	20	18	23	21	19	24	22	20	18	23	21	19	24	22
Wed	23	21	19	24	22	20	25	23	21	19	24	22	20	25	23
Thu	24	22	20	25	23	21	26	24	22	20	25	23	21	26	24
Fri	25	23	21	26	24	22	27	25	23	21	26	24	22	27	25
Sat	26	24	22	27	25	23	28	26	24	22	27	25	23	28	26
Sun	27	25	23	28	26	24	29	27	25	23	28	26	24	29	27
Mon	28	26	24	29	27	25	30	28	26	24	29	27	25	30	28
Tue	29	27	25	30	28	26	-	29	27	25	30	28	26	-	29
Wed	30	28	26	-	29	27	-	30	28	26	-	29	27	-	30
Thu	-	29	27	-	30	28	-	-	29	27	-	30	28	-	-
Fri	-	30	28	-	-	29	-	-	30	28	-	-	29	-	-
Sat	-	-	29	-	-	30	-	-	-	29	-	-	30	-	-
Sun	-	-	30	-	-	-	-	-	-	30	-	-	-	-	-

Messrs A.E. Bloomfield & J.R. Chruch

While doing the research for this paper, I came across two other studies that point to the year 2004 as the date when our Lord will return. One of these studies also points to 1997 as the year the rapture will occur. Both studies were done by very competent and respected scholars whose work should be carefully considered. While both authors believe Scripture teaches that no one can know the exact timing of the Parousia, and each is careful to emphasize that he is not "setting a date", each scholar's work clearly supports the conclusions I have presented in this paper. The following is a short summary of the work done by these men.

The first study is presented on pages 44-54 of the book **"The End of the Days"** by Arthur E. Bloomfield. Bloomfield gathers information from Leviticus, Ezekiel, 2 Chronicles, Jeremiah and Isaiah to develop an extremely interesting theory that intrigues me more each time I consider it.

In Ezekiel 3:24 - 4:17 we are told that Israel will be besieged for 390 years and that Judah will suffer the same fate for an additional 40 years. Much has been written about this dramatized prophecy. However, there is no consensus regarding how the passage should be understood. The prophecy indicates that Israel will be under siege for 430 years and yet there is no clear period in history that would precisely fulfil this passage. Bloomfield's theory is that the siege Ezekiel prophesied began in 586 B.C. when Jerusalem fell to the Babylonians. This period of captivity lasted for 70 years, and was prophesied by Jeremiah:

> **Jeremiah 25:11:** *"And this whole land shall be a desolation and a horror, and these nations shall serve the king of Babylon seventy years."*

> **Jeremiah 29:10:** *"For thus says the Lord, 'When seventy years have been completed for Babylon, I will visit you and fulfill my good word to you, to bring you back to this place."*

Note that Jeremiah does not prophesy that Israel's *"siege"* would end after 70 years. Israel would continue to be in conflict with the Gentile nations and therefore *"under siege"* until the completion of the 430 years. Jeremiah's prophecy only says that for the first 70 years of this siege the Jews will *"serve the king of Babylon"* and then return to their land. Scholars debate about that period of Israel's history fulfilling Jeremiah's prophecy. However, several scholars, including Sir Robert Anderson, understand it to be the 70 years between the destruction of the temple (approximately 586 B.C.) and the finishing of the rebuilt temple (approximately 516 B.C.) A close reading of 2 Chronicles 36:20-23, Ezra 1 and Isaiah 44:28 makes it quite clear, I believe, that Anderson's understanding is correct and Jeremiah's 70 years was indeed the period the temple laid desolate. At the end of the 70 years of Jeremiah's prophecy, Israel would have had an additional 360 years of "siege" to yet endure, however, since the Jews did not all obey God and return to Israel (less than 50,000 returned), God increased the years of discipline they had left by sevenfold. Moses prophesied in Leviticus this would happen:

> **Leviticus 26:17-18:** *"And I will set My face against you so that you shall be struck down before your enemies; and those who hate you shall rule over you, and you shall flee when no one is pursuing you. If also after these things, you do not obey Me, then I will punish you seven times more for your sins."*

Scholars comment that Leviticus 26 and Ezekiel 3-4 are very closely related prophesies. Greenberg, for instance, comments that the *"affinities with Leviticus 26 are most pronounced"* and *"all indications are of Ezekiel's dependence upon Leviticus 26"* (page 127). The phraseology used in Ezekiel's prophecy is strikingly parallel to the passage in Leviticus and thus Bloomfield's linking the two is, I believe, accurate and appropriate.

Bloomfields's theory is that Israel's 360 years of remaining time to be under siege was increased to 2,500 years (360 x 7). The siege against Israel and her conflict with the nations will not end until Jesus returns to be King and according to Bloomfield's theory, that will be 2,500 years after 516 B.C. - *"about A.D. 2004"* (page 54).

J.R. Church is another scholar who's work points, I believe, to a correct date for the Lord's return as well as the correct date for the rapture. Church is adamant he is not "setting a date". However, his intriguing book is clearly asking and attempting to answer questions about the timing of end time events. Incidentally, I object to the term "date setting". The term implies the "date setter" is setting a specific date rather than attempting to discover a date that has been set by God. I believe God will perform His will according to a specific timetable He has laid out and while many Christians maintain we cannot know God's timing, there are sincere and knowledgeable Christians who believe otherwise. Possibly I am making a semantical argument, but I want to establish that this paper is not "setting dates". This paper is an attempt to find dates God has set.

In Church's book **"Hidden Prophecies In the Psalms"** he details his theory that the Psalms each represent a different sequential year of the 20th and 21st centuries. Church believes Psalm 1 provides information about the year 1901, the 2nd Psalm 1902, the 48th 1948 etc. When I first became aware of his work, I was, of course, quite skeptical; however, I now believe he may have discovered a very remarkable truth. One must carefully read Church's work to understand it properly, since it is complex and the arguments he presents are often quite subtle. It is a work that must be studied to be understood. However, when one gives it the considerable attention it deserves, it reveals an amazing and original theory that is exceptionally well researched, and I believe, quite tenable. Whether or not Church's theory will be ultimately proven correct or not I do not know; however, I believe there is considerable merit to it, and I know it supports the work I have done.

According to Church's theory, the 97th Psalm should give us a glimpse of events that will happen in 1997. Note the following phrases that are taken from this Psalm:

Verse 2: *"Clouds and thick darkness surround Him;"*

Verse 4: *"His lightnings lit up the world;*
The earth saw and trembled."

Verse 6   *"And all the peoples have seen His glory."*

Verse 10:   *".... the Lord,*
         Who preserves the souls of His godly ones;
         He delivers them from the hand of the wicked."

Although one cannot take the above verses in isolation and definitively claim they speak about the rapture, those who are familiar with Biblical phraseology should agree they remind us of other passages which speak of our Lord's return for His followers. Chruch understands this Psalm may point to 1997 as the rapture date and he makes the following remarks:

> *"A fascinating description of His glorious appearing is actually given in Psalm 97 ..... Again, that is not to say that His coming will be in 1997. We can only point out that these psalms seem to set a TREND for those events which will lead up to our Saviour's return."* **(Hidden Prophecies in the Psalms,** page 23.)

The 104th Psalm (2004 A.D.) also reminds us of Scripture that speaks about the return of Christ. One needs to study the background work Church has done to follow some of his statements about this Psalm since his opinions are often based upon how the Psalms interrelate with other books of the Bible. Church's research has led him to make the following statements about the 104th Psalm:

> **Page 295:** *"This fourth occurrence of the phrase, Bless the LORD, O my soul compares with the Mosaic book of Numbers and describes the coming of Christ at the conclusion of the Tribulation in power and great glory."*

> **Pages 296-297:** *"The number 104 is comprised of the Hebrew letters 'kop' and 'daleth', root of the word 'kadad', meaning 'to bow the head, to bow before God'. In that day, ... every knee shall bow, and every tongue shall swear ..... allegiance to Him! In that day, all that are against him shall be ashamed (Isaiah 45:23-24)."*

Page 296: *"Verse 35 also begins the first in a series of four Hallelujahs which declare the end of this section of the Psalms - that portion called the Numbers book. These Hallelujahs compare with the four Hallelujahs of Revelation 19:1, 3, 4 and 6."*

The Hallelujahs of Revelation 19 are shouts of acclamation that herald the return of Christ to be King. The return of Jesus will end the Great Tribulation. He will wipe away our tears, and every knee shall bow and every tongue confess that Jesus Christ is Lord!

Bibliography

Anderson, Sir Robert. **The Coming Prince.**
Grand Rapids: Kregel Publications, 1975

Archer, Gleason L. **The Expositor's Bible Commentary.**
Frank E. Gaebelein, General Editor, Grand Rapids; Zondervan, 1985

Baldwin, Joyce G. **The Tyndale Old Testament Commentaries, Daniel.**
D.J. Wiseman, Downers Grove, IL: Inter-varsity Press, 1978.

Bloomfield, Arthur E. **The End of the Days.**
Minneapolis: Bethany House Publishers, 1961

Church, J.R. **Hidden Prophecies in the Psalms.**
Oklahoma City: Prophecy Publications, 1986. Revised 1990

Goldingay, John E. **Word Biblical Commentary.**
Dallas: Word Books, 1989

Greenberg, Moshe. **The Anchor Bible, Ezekiel 1-20.**
Garden City, New York: Doubleday & Company Inc, 1983

Hartman, Louis F. & Alexander A. Di Lelle. **The Anchor Bible, The Book of Daniel.** New York: Doubleday, 1977

Humphreys, Colin J. & Waddington, W.G. **"Dating the Crucifixion".**
Nature, Volume 306, 22/29 December 1983

Jeffrey, Grant R. **Armageddon, Appointment with Destiny.**
New York: Bantam Books, 1990

Keil, Carl Friedrich. **Biblical Commentary on the Book of Daniel.**
Trans M.G. Easton, Grand Rapids: Eerdmans, 1955

Leupold, H.C. **Exposition of Daniel.**
Grand Rapids: Baker Book House. Reprinted 1969

Morris, Henry. **The Genesis Record.** Grand Rapids: Baker Book House and San Diego: Master Books, 1976

Newton, Sir Isaac. **Observations Upon the Prophecies of Daniel and the Apocalypse of St. John.** Cave Junction, Oregon: Oregon Institute of Science and Medicine, 1991 (reprint). Library of Congress. Catalogue Number 91-074116. ISBN 0-942487-02-8

Rosenthal, Marvin. **The Pre-wrath Rapture of the Church.** Nashville: Thomas Nelson Publishers, 1990

Vallowe, Ed F. **Biblical Mathematics.** Forest Park, Georgia: Ed. F. Vallowe Evangelistic Association, 1992

Walvoord, John F. **Daniel The Key to Prophetic Revelation.** Chicago: Moody Press, 1971

Possible Confirmations Subsequent to First Printing

Subsequent to the first printing of this paper, it seems that two rather remarkable confirmations have occurred. Both were brought to my attention by a friend of mine from New York who has helped me with calendar research and several other matters of chronology important to the writing of this paper. He was the first person outside my family to receive a copy of this paper and he immediately informed me that Jesus' ascension date was May 14th 33 A.D. He is extremely knowledgeable in the field of ancient chronology and calendars, and he believes strongly that Humphreys and Waddington's work is definitive regarding the date Jesus was crucified. Humphreys and Waddington, mentioned on page 49 of this paper, have concluded Jesus was crucified on April 3rd 33 A.D. Anyone wanting a copy of the article which details their research may write to me for a copy, however, suffice it to say, the question of when Jesus died has, to the satisfaction of numerous experts, now been definitively settled. It is almost certain Jesus died on April 3rd 33 A.D., and if that is the case, then He arose on Sunday, April 5th 33 A.D., remained on earth for 40 days (Acts 1:3) and was translated (raptured) on May 14th 33 A.D. (Acts 1:9-11)! Jesus, it appears, was raptured on May 14th, the same day on the calendar this paper concludes the faithful will be raptured. One further note: Ed. F. Vallowe, in his highly respected work, **Biblical Mathematics,** maintains the number 14 is a number associated with salvation and deliverance.

The second possible confirmation is the coming Hale-Bopp comet. My friend from New York was the first to inform me about this great comet which scientists expect to appear in the spring of 1997. Hale-Bopp will be at its brightest during April, the month before I believe the rapture will happen. This comet is going to be a spectacular event and early indications are it could be 10 times larger and 100 times brighter than Halley's comet! The Bible prophesies there will be signs in the heavens during the last days, and surely Hale-Bopp is a soon-to-arrive fulfilment of these prophecies. It could be that Hale-Bopp is a sign pointing to the rapture.

❖ ❖ ❖